Toddler Troubles

Coping with Your Under-5s

Jo Douglas

Chartered Clinical Psychologist

JOHN WILEY & SONS, LTD

Other Wiley Editorial Offices

John Wiley & Sons Inc., 111 River Street, Hoboken, NJ 07030, USA

Jossey-Bass, 989 Market Street, San Francisco, CA 94103-1741, USA

Wiley-VCH Verlag GmbH, Boschstr. 12, D-69469 Weinheim, Germany

John Wiley & Sons Australia Ltd, 33 Park Road, Milton, Queensland 4064, Australia

John Wiley & Sons (Asia) Pte Ltd, 2 Clementi Loop #02-01, Jin Xing Distripark,
Singapore
129809

John Wiley & Sons (Canada) Ltd, 22 Worcester Road, Etobicoke, Ontario M9W 1L1

Library of Congress Cataloging-in-Publication Data
Douglas, Jo, 1950–
    Toddler troubles : coping with your under-5s / Jo Douglas.
        p. cm.—(Family matters)
    Includes bibliographical references and index.
    ISBN 0-470-84686-0 (alk. paper)
    1. Toddlers. 2. Toddlers—Care. 3. Toddlers—Psychology. I. Title.
    II. Family matters (John Wiley & Sons)

    HQ774.5 .D68 2002
    649'.122—dc21   2002072369

British Library Cataloguing in Publication Data
A catalogue record for this book is available from the British Library

ISBN 0–470–84686–0

Project management by Originator, Gt Yarmouth, Norfolk (typeset in 11.5/13pt Imprint)
Printed and bound in Great Britain by Biddles Ltd, Guildford and King's Lynn
This book is printed on acid-free paper responsibly manufactured from sustainable
forestry, in which at least two trees are planted for each one used for paper production.

Toddler Troubles

Because your family matters ...

Family Matters is a new series from Wiley highlighting topics that are important to the everyday lives of family members. Each book tackles a common problem or difficult situation, such as teenage troubles, new babies or problems in relationships, and provides easily understood advice from authoritative professionals. The *Family Matters* series is designed to provide expert advice to ordinary people struggling with everyday problems and bridges the gap between the professional and client. Each book also offers invaluable help to practitioners as extensions to the advice they can give in sessions, and helps trainees to understand the issues clients face.

Titles in the series:

Contents

Foreword

Toddlers have a very busy life: there are so many rules to learn, so many skills to acquire, so many people to meet, so many places and things to explore. No wonder toddler-hood is thought of as a 'sensitive' stage of development, with a long psychological 'reach' into adolescence and even adulthood, especially when things go badly wrong. Small children can be demanding and exhausting. Next minute they're all sweet and loveable again. Coping with the ups and downs of looking after the under-5s can often leave parents feeling confused and guilty. It can, indeed, be a 'troublesome' time as the title of this informative and fascinating book suggests. However, it needn't earn its sobriquet 'the terrible twos' if parents are strategically positive in their outlook and tactically knowledgeable in their child-care – deciding from the outset to enjoy rather than endure their child's pre-school years. And this is precisely where the author's guidance to mothers and fathers is so valuable. Jo Douglas, a parent and clinical psychologist, working with families for over 25 years, understands how hard it is when small children refuse to eat or sleep. In *Toddler Troubles*, she provides effective ideas for handling common problems in family life, like temper tantrums, endless questions, toilet training, eating and sleeping, and coping with endlessly quarrelling brothers and sisters. She writes in a readable, unpatronising and jargon-free style that 'speaks' empathically to parents about their concerns and worries in a manner that should instil confidence in even the most anxious or inexperienced parents.

Of course, there are many self-help books in the bookshops on raising children. But to find one that informs parents (on the basis of hard evidence) about what they might actually *do and say* in particular circumstances is extremely rare. The author draws on years of clinical contact with challenging pre-schoolers to provide answers to issues ranging from the effects of having a baby on the mother's self-esteem and on marital relationships, the consequences of early separations and divorce, to the day-to-day and not-so-common childhood problems that challenge hard-pressed families.

Toddler Troubles has applications for all young children. Jo Douglas's major themes are about the power of 'positive parenting' and the effectiveness of creative thinking and behavioural problem-solving in coping with the vicissitudes of raising children. She has succeeded brilliantly by her 'positive' writing and a feeling for the dilemmas of parenthood. I heartily recommend her book to you.

Martin Herbert
Emeritus Professor of Clinical Child Psychology
Exeter University

About the author

Jo Douglas has worked with families and children as a Clinical Psychologist for the last 27 years. She worked for 25 years at Great Ormond Street Hospital in London where she established and directed a Day Centre treatment programme for young children with severe and chronic eating problems. She was latterly Head of the Psychology Service there.

   She is well known for her work on management of sleep problems in young children which she carried out with Dr Naomi Richman and which produced the first book she co-authored *My Child Won't Sleep* (1984). Since that time she has written extensively, including books for parents *Coping with Young Children* (1984) and *Is my Child Hyperactive?* (1991), and for professionals *Behaviour Problems in Young Children* (1989) and *Psychology and Nursing Children* (1993). Her primary interest has always been in helping parents of young children manage the wide range of worries and concerns that develop as children grow and change. She has lectured extensively and trained many health visitors,

nurses and doctors in behavioural management techniques for parents with young children through the
courses she organised at the Institute of Child Health in
London.

She is now an independent psychologist and is
enjoying life seeing families and children for assessment
and treatment and also writing. She has always tried to
keep a balance in her work life with a commitment to
home life and her family. Working part-time when the
children were young was her way of managing her own
needs but also meeting the needs of the family. She was
lucky in having a very fulfilling job at Great Ormond
Street Hospital, which allowed her to develop her
interests. The stimulating environment there of professional colleagues was a fertile ground for exploration of
clinical ideas and approaches to treatment.

She has been married for 25 years and has two
daughters, aged 17 years and 22 years, plus a dog, five
fish, a rabbit and a guinea pig. Her husband has been
her main support throughout and has encouraged her as
a wife, a mother and a psychologist.

Acknowledgements

It is impossible to acknowledge everyone who has had an influence on me during the course of my life that has resulted in the writing of this book. Friends, colleagues, patients and relatives all have contributed ideas, examples and memories that I draw on when writing.

I would like to thank Dr Jake Mackinnon for spending valuable time reading the manuscript and providing comments, editing and checking on the medical information. It's great to know that we both think the same way. Also thanks to Vivien Ward for suggesting that I might like to have a go at writing this book.

I would also like to thank the families that I have seen over my clinical career as a clinical psychologist at Great Ormond Street Hospital. We have learned some of this together and I hope that I have been able to provide a small element of direction and optimism in their lives. My colleagues at the hospital, including Richard Lansdown, Bryan Lask, Roy Howarth, Naomi Richman and Philip Graham, were all formative influences and gave me the freedom and confidence to develop my ideas. Also thanks to Peter Hill for supporting me over the past two years in setting up a private practice and sending me so many fascinating cases.

My special thanks go to my family, and in particular my husband Robin who has supported me throughout my career and in the care of our two girls Alex and Amanda who are now well on their way to leaving the family. It's strange to think that I am writing about pre-school children, remembering many of the early times in their early lives, while managing life with an adolescent and a young adult. But it's been illuminating to recognise how the ideas about being a parent in the early years carry on right through to adolescence, with a few modifications!

Also, sincere thanks to my parents who set me on the path of psychology and gave me the courage and confidence to meet and rise to the challenges when they came.

As always, it is difficult to decide how to refer to the child in a book such as this. I have opted for the traditional choice of using he/him rather than swapping throughout with her/she. This will really irritate those of you who have little girls, as I have, so please accept my apologies and try to substitute your child's gender throughout. This also does not imply that only boys have these problems, girls can be just as difficult.

Being a parent

You have probably picked up this book because you are already concerned about some aspect of your toddler's behaviour and want to think about how best to handle some of the difficult situations that you find yourself in. Welcome to the club. You are not alone and your child is not unusual. Being a parent is often difficult, worrying, and confusing. How do you know what is the best course of action? We often feel guilty; we are unsure of how to react; we worry that we are the cause of the problem. Sometimes we feel exhausted, angry, resentful, exasperated and worn down with the responsibility and daily drudgery of caring for young children. The pleasure they can give is unparalleled but the strain and continual demands for attention, love and care can wear you out. Being a parent is not easy. The wonder and excitement of the birth of a new baby rapidly can be replaced with worry and uncertainty about how to manage his crying, his feeding and his sleeping. This little person suddenly has demands that you have to interpret and meet. You are responsible for the first time for another life. You are

responsible for his care, his growth and development.
How do you know what to do? Does it come naturally?
Do you always know how best to cope with situations?
Generally we all muddle along with a mixture of advice
from our parents, our relatives, our friends, books, TV,
newspapers and magazines, and hope it works out. We do
our best, we love our children and hope that our love will
overcome any mistakes that we make along the way. This
book is the result of the experience of being a parent of two
girls, and of the experience of being in clinical practice as a
child clinical psychologist for 25 years, working with
parents and their young children. This is not a book of
answers as no-one can provide the right solution for all
problems. Each child is an individual like no other, and
each family that a child is born into has its own history. I
hope this book will provide you with ways of thinking
about situations that arise with your toddlers so that you
can find the right solution for you and for your child.

Understanding your child

Your baby is born unable to speak English and unable to
tell you what he needs and wants. So what do you do? You
start guessing and trying to understand what all the wrig-
gles, noises, cries and screams mean. Already you are
imposing on your baby your view of what is the matter.
Where do you get this view from?

During your pregnancy you may have tried to guess
whether the bump was a boy or a girl. Each sex brings its
own expectations and hopes. You or your partner may
desperately want a boy and when your little girl is born
how do you feel? Your emotions and hopes will dramatically impact on how you respond to your baby. Disappoint-

ment can grow to detachment, positive anticipation may turn to blame and rejection. Or it may just take a short while to adjust and learn to love the new baby. You may have already provided your baby with a full personality before birth. 'He's so irritating, he always kicks when I'm trying to go to sleep.' 'She is so lively I think she's going to be a handful.' 'If I sing to her every day and listen to lots of music she is bound to be musical.' Babies often embody the hopes of our own missed opportunities. How many times have you heard others say, 'I want him to have everything I never had'. This tells you far more about the parent than the baby.

The moment your baby is born everyone starts telling you their view of who he is, his characteristics, his personality, his good points, his bad points, who he looks like. The nurse in the delivery room says, 'You've got a great footballer here, look how he's kicking!' Both of you will look for family characteristics. You may think that your newborn is terribly ugly and not what you expected at all. He may have dark hair and you expected light hair, or he may have a big nose. It can take time to get used to the look of your newborn and to get to know him as yours. Or you may fall in love at first sight and think he is the most beautiful baby in the world. Your feelings and expectations at birth will already set the scene for how you interpret your baby's behaviour. One mother told me that the midwife told her, 'You've got a right one here, he's really going to give you a hard time'. This little boy was a very lively and excitable toddler and had always been a handful. I wonder why?

When you become a parent you inflict on your baby your own interpretation of his behaviour. This is bound up with your own childhood experiences, your experiences of relationships as a child and an adult and the way you see the world. If you are the type of person who readily feels criticised by others, or who feels others are always blaming you, then you might be more inclined to interpret your baby's crying as indicating that you are a bad parent or that you are no good at understanding what is the matter. The sense of judgement that you feel inside can build up into resentment and anger at the crying and lead into a spiral of tension and inability to separate the baby's needs from your own feelings. I think most parents have felt like this at some time. We all carry a sense of insecurity around with us; we want to be liked and thought to be clever, good and attractive, even though we damp down these feelings much of the time and pretend that they are not there. Your baby can reveal these feelings at times of stress and you may be astonished at how intense your sense of being attacked or undermined by your baby's demands can be. 'Why can't I understand what he wants?' 'I don't know what to do.' 'Why can't I satisfy his demands?' 'I feel so helpless and inadequate.' Some parents will turn this onto the baby and blame him for being difficult rather than blaming themselves for not coping. 'He's a really bad baby, he's always crying and never seems to accept being settled.' 'I hate him when he cries.'

This is all starting to sound a bit complicated, but really it boils down to the importance of being aware of yourself and what makes you tick. Being a parent brings out into the open your thoughts about others, your reactions to others' behaviour, your expectations and interpretations of how others react to you, your insecurities, your strengths, your temper. Being aware of yourself and your feelings and the reasons for your reactions will help in understanding your baby. How much of what you feel is to do with you and how much is it to do with your baby?

Your emotional state will dramatically affect how you react to your baby. If you are depressed you will be unavailable emotionally and cut off from your baby. If you are unhappy you may be irritable, angry and volatile in your reactions to your baby. If you are a worrier you may be over-intrusive, over-protective and smothering of your baby. We know that high levels of emotional arousal stop us thinking effectively; it also stops us problem-solving and understanding events around us. A parent who is highly aroused therefore is often unable to understand their baby's behaviour. We need to be calm and in control in order to analyse a situation and react appropriately. This is easier said than done. How many parents can really say that they analyse each situation coolly and calmly? One way through this is to focus on your baby's needs rather than your own. We need to try and put our own feelings aside and watch the baby carefully, trying to understand how the baby is feeling. Your baby is dependent on you to interpret the world for him, to contain his feelings, to ameliorate his stress and meet his needs. He is busy trying to understand and predict events that happen to him, and you are the main way in which he can learn to anticipate and control the world.

Am I a good parent?

We all want to be good parents, but what does that mean? Providing a safe home, good food, good health, a loving environment, a stimulating education and opportunities to socialise and play.

But beyond this we want to know if we are saying and doing the right things? Is there a right way to bring up children? Are we doing psychological and emotional damage by saying something hurtful or punishing our children? When we look back on parenting advice over the last 100 years, there have been great changes in attitudes and patterns of child care and child rearing. There

are differences across different ethnic groups and societies
around the world. Clearly there is no one right answer,
but patterns of child care develop in response to the needs
of the society that the child is born into. At present most
children in British society are born into a nuclear family
structure with limited contact with the extended family
and dependence on the state for health, education and
social support. There have been dramatic changes in the
structure of family life as the incidence of divorce has
increased and many children are born into and grow up
in complex stepfamily structures. How we manage
divorce and reconstituted family life is an issue for many
parents and children.

We expect and demand perfect babies, which is resulting in an increase of up to 20% in the number of Caesarean
section deliveries. We are all important individuals in a
society that tries to support human rights, equality and
freedom of speech. So we need to think as parents about
what are the requirements to grow up in such a society and
be successful. Think about how you view the Chinese
requirement only to have one child per family. How do
you think this will affect the next generation and how they
behave and socialise?

Within each family you need to reflect on the values
that you think are important to you. Only then can you
consider how you wish to bring up your children, what
behaviour you would like to see, what values you wish to
instil and pass on to future generations. Do you know your
own values? Do you know what motivates you? One thing
that seems clear for many parents is that financial and
occupational success is not the only important feature of
life, even though it takes up so much time and effort.
Fulfilling relationships, happy family life, caring for
each other and love are so much more important and
gratifying at the end of the day. So we need to consider
how best to help our children grow up with a sense of care

for each other, to be able to make enduring and satisfying relationships with each other, to have good friends and eventually make long-lasting adult relationships so that the next generation is assured and well cared-for.

Doubts and uncertainties

Being a parent is learning how to cope with uncertainty. Adapting to another personality as it grows and changes is a challenge. Many parents find that as they learn to cope with and adapt to one stage of development their child has already moved onto the next stage. You just manage your day around your infant having two naps a day and then suddenly you find he is onto one nap a day and lunch won't fit in because he's either too tired to eat or it's too early or late. At least it keeps you on your toes and at no time can you grow complacent.

Guilt

Motherhood is a non-stop guilt trip. You can often feel that whatever you do is wrong in someone's eyes. This is partly to do with the balancing act that many women experience trying to combine work or career with parenthood, the needs of different children, the needs of children versus partner, and needs of children and partner against self. Guilt is a very destructive emotion and can be incapacitating.

   To work or not to work is often one of the most difficult decisions mothers of young children make. We have a

very powerful ability to affirm our own decisions by
seeking out parallel decisions that match our own and
ignoring evidence to the contrary. If you decide that you
need to go to work while your child is a preschooler for
your own sanity, or that you need to for serious financial
reasons, then you should acknowledge that reason to
yourself and make the best alternative care arrangements
for your children that you can afford. The most destructive process is to go back to work and then feel guilty that
you should be at home. It will destroy you. It will destroy
your relationship with your children as you indulge them
in recompense for not being there during the day. It will
destroy your work. Mothers who feel guilty for going to
work may keep their children up at night and then feel
resentful and exhausted as they themselves do not get
enough sleep to perform well during the day.

Fathers coming in late from work may expect the
children to be kept up so that they can see them and
proceed to get them playful and over-excited before they
are expected to settle to sleep. If your needs are becoming
more important than the needs of your child, then it will
lead to disruption, confused emotional messages and more
guilt.

Be clear about your decisions and the reasons for
them. Lists of pros and cons will be helpful but must be
truthful. There are always two sides to a decision, so make
the best one you can at the time and in those circumstances. You can always change it later if you find out
that it does not work or is wrong for you and your
family. But don't make a decision and then carry on re-
gretting it but do nothing about it.

Alternatively, guilt can make you feel completely in-
capacitated and unable to make any decision. This is often
the route to depression as you feel out of control of your
life, unsure of your decisions and unsatisfied with your
actions. Sometimes this is bound up with your own

ideal view of a super-mum. The sort of person who can do finger painting and not worry about the mess, who reads stories repeatedly without getting bored, who involves their child in cooking and cleaning without getting irritated about the delays and continual questions, who has unbounded energy and enthusiasm, who never uses the TV as a toddler occupier, who enrols their toddler into all of the right classes and is teaching the Suzuki violin! This super-mum does not exist. She is a combination of all of the things we think we ought to do and so the sum is greater than the parts. All of the self-statements that include 'I should ...', 'I ought ...', 'I must ...' create an internal pressure that can lead to resentment and reduced motivation. If we think of statements that include 'I want to ...', 'I can do ...', 'It would be fun to ...', 'I would like to ...', it is easy to see how our attitude can change and we feel more motivated, more interested and able to cope. The shift is in thinking about who you are and how you feel. Being realistic about your capabilities is the first step in making better decisions about how to manage your life and your family. Your own assessment of yourself will identify both good and bad points. So rather than feeling guilty about everything all of the time, you start to recognise what you can do and perhaps also identify something that you would like to change. Rather than saying to yourself, 'I ought to take them swimming', but feeling guilty because you never go, you might recognise, 'I hate swimming so I'll take them to the park instead. They can learn to swim in a class when they are older.'

Working together and sharing

Two heads are generally better than one when trying to problem-solve and make decisions. Sadly many mothers

seek help and advice on their own for their children's
problems when in fact the father may have helpful comments and ideas. When I first started helping parents with
their children's sleep problems I would invite both
parents along to the first session and many a time I was
met with the comment from the fathers about how nice it
was to be invited and considered as having a view. Fathers
were usually essential in deciding on the best course of
action for managing the problem and would often
commit themselves to helping out in ways that their
partner had not considered. Fathers are so often left out
of discussions around young children, partly because they
are at work and cannot take time off, or perhaps because
mothers do not let them have a say. You may find this
unfair, but just think how many times you have seen a
friend not let the baby's father change a nappy in case
they do it wrong, or hover over his shoulder telling him
what to do until he gives up and leaves it to her.

Sharing child care and responsibilities is a very important part of parenting and often needs very careful
consideration. The rot can start with breast-feeding
when fathers can feel left out because they cannot calm
the baby by feeding. The 'special relationship' that seems
to develop with the breast-feeding mother has exclusive
membership and fathers may feel they have no role. Make
sure that you check out each others' feelings about this
and try to understand how the other partner feels. Try to
be clear about your own position and learn to negotiate to
meet your own needs. One mother had such problems
during the initial breast-feeding weeks, due to sore
nipples, that she could only bear to feed her baby while
sitting cradled by her partner with him enouraging her to
carry on. She came through the difficult period and
realised how important he had been to her in supporting
the whole process.

The father has a very important role in the family,

particularly in supporting the mother. Winnicott (1998) visualised the baby as being held by the mother while the mother is held and supported by the father who is in turn held and supported by society. This conceptualisation of family life does provide one insight into the dependency of parents and how they take on complementary roles in order to provide a safe and caring environment in which to rear children.

Resentment towards each other can build up very quickly as you adopt the new roles of parents. You must talk and share your feelings as you adjust and cope with the new demands. Some mothers report that their partners are selfish and uncaring while they try to cope with the baby, while fathers report their partners as ignoring and excluding them. It is always more helpful to think about the other person's needs as well as your own. You will rapidly find that you understand how they feel and a compromise or a negotiation can be reached. Recognising that you both are struggling with the new roles and responsibilities is necessary in order to accommodate the other's views. We all feel that we need to be cared for and treated as special, and the last thing that a new mother will be thinking about is how her partner needs to be looked after as well as the new baby. But if she wishes to be cared for she also needs to do some caring in return. Try to reverse the situation in your mind and see how you would feel in your partner's shoes.

Negotiating

Once you have understood what is going wrong and why you feel so bad, it is time to consider how to negotiate to have your needs met and the situation to alter a bit so that

you feel supported and appreciated. 'To negotiate' means
to work or talk with others to achieve an agreement or
settlement. The process of negotiation, therefore, needs
to be constructive and amiable rather than confrontational
and assertive. 'Why don't you ever have the children so I
can have some peace and quiet?' or 'They're your children
too; why don't you ever come home on time to see them
before bed?' are not negotiations. Neither is 'Why can't
you keep the kids quiet when I come in, I'm so tired and
stressed after work'. We can often think about what we
want out of a negotiation but stating just our own view will
result in a confrontation rather than a mutually satisfying
solution.

The basis of a successful negotiation is a win–win
situation where both parties benefit from the solution.
This needs an understanding of each person's point of
view and the raising of several solutions that could meet
the problem. Start by stating the problem, 'Can we talk
about what happens in the evening when I come in from
work? It seems to be a problem time and we all seem to be
getting angry. We need to think about how to manage this
pressure point.' It is already stated as a joint issue that
needs two heads to solve. Recognition of the stresses
that affect both parents at this point of the day should
be shared, focusing on owning your own needs rather
than saying what you think the other partner should do,
and covertly blaming them for not doing it. 'I'm exhausted when I come in and just want time to get
changed out of work-clothes, have a drink and calm
down. I need some peace.' 'I'm exhausted by 6 p.m., I
need to get the supper made and the children are tired
and fractious and need a bath. I need some help.' With
needs clearly laid out it is much easier to try and find a
solution together. You might decide on – 'Let's lock our-
selves in the kitchen and have a drink or a cup of tea and
forget all the things we have to do for half an hour' or 'I

can keep the kids away from you for half an hour if you will then bath them and help put them to bed before we have our supper.' Or 'I know they'll be excited when I get in so I'll keep them occupied while you cook supper, and then we can relax together'. You both need to gain from the solution so sharing the responsibility of being parents is very important.

Who am I?

Once you have children you develop another identity – you are a parent. You've never been this before and often you have no clue as to whether you are going to be a good or a bad parent, whether you will like having children or not, whether you will reject or accept this new identity. You have your identity as you: the person who grew up in your own family. You are a son or a daughter, a brother or a sister. You are the person who had an education, the person who has a job or a career. You are also a partner in a relationship, whether this be husband or wife, a cohabitee, or a lover. Now you are in addition a mother or a father and suddenly your responsibilities multiply and your attitude to life takes a sudden jolt.

Women who give up careers or satisfying jobs to take care of their children lose one identity while gaining another. No wonder it is a 'life event'. The adaptation and adjustment is considerable and no wonder new parents are often stressed and unclear about who they are and what they want to do. Your life changes from living in the adult world, having adult conversations, enjoying adult pastimes, making important work decisions, being decisive and clear-thinking. Suddenly you are at home with an unpredictable tiny person who yells at

you a lot, who you have to think for when you've had no
experience or training in which nappy to buy, how to feed
and burp a baby, how to solve cradle cap, what to do about
nappy rash and how to tell when he's ill. The number of
decisions or guesses you make on a daily basis are
enormous in a whole new world of conflicting information. You try to rapidly absorb all of this new knowledge,
make contact with other parents, talk about which is the
best washing powder or how to get poo marks off baby
clothes. Gradually your life is overwhelmed with your
new identity. You have to care for and protect this new
life. Your knowledge about the range of baby toys and
types of buggies grows exponentially but your knowledge
of office gossip, how your work project is progressing,
which are the new restaurants to try and colleagues'
views on the daily news is diminishing rapidly. You find
that slowly you become a 'mum' who hasn't had time to
read the newspaper and so doesn't know what is happening in the wider world; who never has the energy or uninterrupted time to read a good novel any more; who
never has the chance to dress up and look good as the
baby always possets down your back; who can't go out
to dance or eat or go to the cinema because of no available
babysitter / the expense of a babysitter / demand breast
feeding / guilt about leaving the baby.

Some women love this time. They have desperately
wanted to have a baby for all sorts of reasons. They
enjoy the process of motherhood and revel in the break
from a boring job. They embrace this new identity with
fervour and don't look back. They love being at home,
talking with other mothers. They want to care for others
and do not feel whole or satisfied unless they can think
outside themselves and put others needs before their own.
That is marvellous for them; but it may not be for you.
You may feel depressed, flat, bored, uninterested and
rather irritable without fully realising why. You've lost

touch with yourself and you need to re-establish the balance between your identity as you and your identity as a mother.

Looking after yourself

You need to look after yourself if you are going to look after others. It is easy for mothers of young children to dismiss their own needs while the children's needs are treated as primary. It is time to look at what is happening in your family, to you and to your relationship with your partner.

You may find that you can feel happy only when the children are happy and content. Your feelings have become a reflection of theirs. What has happened to you? Your motherhood identity has totally overtaken you.

What did you enjoy doing and what made you feel good before the children arrived? Did you go to the gym? Did you read books or magazines? Did you take time doing your nails and your hair? Did you go out more? Did you have long and luxurious baths? You can lose contact with these basic good experiences and then feel dissatisfied with your partner for not making you feel good or thinking about what you need. As soon as you sense the thought that he should know how you feel or he should know what you like, you are starting to assume that he can read your mind and you are on very dangerous territory. You may even be placing the responsibility on him to make you feel good when you have forgotten what makes you feel good yourself.

The first step is to list what you used to do that made you feel you, or what used to make you feel good as a woman. Your self-confidence and self-esteem play a large part here. Looking good was probably quite high on the list, so, think about how you used to pamper and take care of yourself. If you've gained weight since the baby, then think about how to lose weight or join a keep-fit class – they all have crèches these days. See it as time for you, and something that you are doing for yourself. Use the time when your child goes to play at a friend's house to enjoy reading a book, do some gardening (if you like it), or even do the ironing (only if you can really feel pleased that you are at peace and uninterrupted). Find events that you can appreciate as being for you even if they are squeezed in during your toddler's daytime nap; don't just use it as time to do a job that needs to be done. Look for positives in the day and pat yourself on the back for your achievements. It may sound a bit sad but sometimes having cleaned the windows, or changed all of the beds can give you a great sense of satisfaction.

Once you have learned to be positive towards yourself and aware of what you need and how to achieve it, then you are in a better position to think about your relationship with your partner.

Looking after your relationship

John, who was feeling rejected and anxious, described how his wife always put the needs of their children first and made him feel bad if he asserted his own needs. If he wanted to take his wife out she made excuses about not being able to get a babysitter; or if they did manage to, she spent the whole evening talking about the children. She never seemed to have time to talk about what happened at his work during the day, while prior to having the children she had always been supportive and helped him make some important work decisions. He felt he was at the bottom of the pile and he wondered what had happened to their relationship.

Maria, who was feeling depressed and over-stressed, described her life as revolving totally around the children. She was the taxi-driver, the cook, the carer, the nurse and the teacher. She never went out with her partner because they had never managed to arrange a babysitter so he tended to go to the pub on his own at the weekend. She could never arrange to see her own female friends during the week as he was unpredictable in his late meetings at work.

In both of these cases the balance in the relationships had been lost and the identity of the partners was at risk of being swamped. One of you has to start the swing back to establishing the balance again. Your love and your relationship was the whole basis for the development of the family and it is vital to keep that alive and kicking. Remember what it was that made you fall in love and want to be with each other.

- What was it that you think your partner liked about you before the children arrived?

- What did you like about your partner before the children arrived?
- Are those special features still present or have they been lost during the submersion in parenthood?
- What did you do together, in the past, that you enjoyed?

One golden rule of thumb is the necessity of making time together for one evening a week when you are adults and no longer parents – go to the cinema or the pub, meet friends or have a meal out without discussing the children. It gives you a chance to dress up, it is something to look forward to and reasserts the importance of your relationship and your care for each other. If your partner seems to have forgotten how to book a table or make a decision about which film to see, don't let your sense of injustice take over, just do it and he will feel pleased that you care enough to make a decision. If it's a film he doesn't like he might be motivated to make the decision next time, or at least discuss it with you. You might even forget for a short while that you are parents – and I'm sure that is perfectly healthy.

Exhaustion

Exhaustion can be physical, mental or emotional. It can result in depression, irritability, uncontrollable frustration and anger. You niggle at your partner, you blame each other, you want to be looked after, you want someone to do something for you. You shout at the children, you don't enjoy being with them, everything you do is a chore and an effort. It is a debilitating condition and must be controlled and managed. It can be phasic, occur at particular times of the day, or be pervasive.

First you should work out which type of exhaustion you have.

- Are you tired because your child is keeping you awake at night?
- Are you exhausted because you are feeling depressed?
- Are you worn out with the physical care of active young children and live on the fourth floor with no lift?
- Are you tired because you are unwell, not eating properly, lacking vitamins?
- Are you tired because you are worried about financial or other problems?
- Are you tired because you are unhappy?
- Are you tired because you are bored?

Once you know why you feel so exhausted you can start to do something about it. If your child has a sleep problem then work out a method that will encourage him to sleep better (see Chapter 7). If you are depressed then use some of the other ideas discussed in this chapter to reflect on what is happening to you, why you are depressed and how to combat it by looking after yourself or your relationship. See your GP to discuss symptoms and he may diagnose postnatal depression. Phasic depression may be to do with time of the day. Many mothers feel tired around the end of the day, 4–5 p.m. One mother managed this by getting into her bed and encouraging all of her children in with her for a cuddle, she would switch on the TV to watch children's programmes for an hour while she relaxed and stopped rushing around the house. It gave her enough space to recharge her batteries for the evening onslaught of meals, bath and bed.

If you feel that you really cannot manage then indicate to your partner that you really need some help and try to get this agreed on a regular basis rather than as crisis management. Otherwise use a relative or friend to help out, pay for some time-limited child care if you can, or treat yourself to having someone to help clean the house.

Set yourself realistic goals and don't try to be super-mum and have a spotless house, immaculate children, freshly home-cooked meals twice a day and the ironing basket always clear. Make sure that you have your prior-ities straight. It is far more important to have had a relaxed and fun bathtime with your children than an irri-table and rushed bathtime but an immaculate kitchen floor. I have a golden rule that, if you are dusting your light bulbs and ironing your knickers, then you have serious problems with priorities and excessively high standards. If standards slip for a few years while your children are young then this is not the end of the world.

Home and work

If you go out to work while you have young children you certainly will have a very full life. It is inevitable that something will give and you need to be clear that compro-mises will have to be made on one side or the other, or on both. There is a sacrifice whatever you do. If you work full-time you are really unlikely to see your children much during the week. You might be home in time for bedtime, but it's possible that your boss may expect you to stay on for the 'normal' long hours of non-parent workers. What do you do about after-hours meetings? Do you say that you cannot stay later than 6 p.m. and risk the flak? You may miss out on after-work chats and drinks, which is when most of the team work is done. Do you leave work undone on your desk because you have to collect the children from their child carer? It is not easy, and no one solution is applicable to everyone. You have to work it out for yourself.

Make a list of pros and cons – it usually results in either a split between financial need and time with the children or career progression and family life. Do you need as much money as you think you do? Is your career really important to you in terms of your self-image and status? Do you need the stimulation of having a job as well as having children?

If you decide that continuing full-time work is the best option, then you need to make clear plans for good-quality child care and work out how much it will cost you. It can match the cost of the additional salary in some families and then you need to work out if it is really worth it. Some parents decide on split responsibilities if one does shift work. Others work out that part-time work for one partner is possible, which helps alleviate guilt about not seeing the children all week.

We talk glibly about quality time rather than quantity of time in order to alleviate our guilt. In fact, how much quality is there when you arrive home tired and frazzled after a long day and traffic jams? At the weekend, how do you manage the weekly shopping and all of the jobs around the house as well as taking your children out, playing with them and being a stimulating quality parent? It really is not possible; something has to give and you need to make sure that it isn't you.

Your primary responsibility is to ensure safe and good alternative child care when you are not available. Your child ideally needs to make close relationships to predictable, caring and warm adults who will be consistent and

available for him. Whether relatives step in, or you send
your child to a child minder or a nursery, or have an au
pair or nanny look after your child in your own house will
depend on your financial circumstances and preferences.
Your child will still make a secure attachment with you
but he must also make attachments to their other carers
and you must be careful about feeling jealous or competitive. The carer you choose is there to replace you
and, if your child does not feel an emotional bond with
them, then it is not a good choice. You need to let this
relationship develop but feel confident that your child also
loves you. You can see that rapid or frequent changing of
single carers will be detrimental to your child's emotional
development, so you need to try and ensure that there is
consistency in any arrangement.

Conclusion

Being a parent is fraught with problems and difficulties.
Keeping a balance for yourself and your partner is important. Your own emotional state will have a significant
impact on your child's emotional state and also on his
behaviour, so you need to be aware of how to keep yourself
strong and in touch with your feelings without being overwhelmed. If you know yourself, you will be better able to
manage your child. Guilt and depression are destructive
feelings so beware of them and work out how to get some
help for yourself. Be realistic about what is possible and
don't drive yourself into the ground.

Topical tips

- Be aware of yourself and your feelings.

- Try to see the world through your baby's eyes.

- Being a parent is learning how to cope with uncertainty.

- Motherhood can feel like a non-stop guilt trip.

- Be realistic about your capabilities in managing your life and your family.

- Recognise what you 'can' do rather than what you 'ought' to do.

- Two heads are better than one in solving problems.

- Successful negotiation is a win–win solution.

- Look after yourself if you are going to look after others.

- Make time to spend with your partner, not just as parents.

2

Being a positive parent

Being a parent is not about how to discipline your children effectively. It is mostly about nurturing their skills, protecting them, understanding their feelings, and helping them cope with the world around them. We need to focus on how we help and teach them. The most effective way of learning is when your teacher is warm, caring and supportive – someone who gives you positive feedback about how well you are doing and helps correct mistakes without being critical. For the first five years of life your child is primarily learning from you.

Practising positive parenting

You are probably feeling unhappy about how stressed you feel by caring for your preschooler. You are shouting more than you mean to, you don't seem to enjoy being with him because of the continual demands; he never

seems to listen to you and doesn't do as he is told. It's time
to improve the quality of your relationship.

Firstly you need to remember what you love about
him rather than thinking of the problems. Write down a
list of all of the things you like and enjoy about your child.
He may be very affectionate, have lovely blond curly hair,
love to look at books, be cuddly, have a good sense of
humour, have a lovely infectious laugh. These are important characteristics as they counter all of the problems you
are coping with, his hyperactivity, his temper tantrums
and his bedwetting. Despite his problems you love him.
Sadly, the problems can start to overshadow the good
points and it is easy to lose sight of the child that you love.

You need to build on the good qualities and improve
your relationship with your child so that you both enjoy
being together. So take some time each day to be with him
with no distractions or other jobs to do and no time pressure. Value and label this time as his 'special time' with you
(Forehand & McMahon, 1981).

- Let him choose the activity and just be there attending to what he is playing, joining in and helping.
  'What a lovely truck.' 'Look how many cars you've
  managed to get in the garage.'
- Praise him, 'That's a lovely tower you've built'; talk
  about what he is doing and touch him positively, a
  pat on the head and quick hug that are not intrusive
  or demanding of affection back.
- Try not to ask questions, make criticisms, give commands or reprimand him during this time; stay
  positive and attentive.

This special time is precious and is time for you to enjoy
being with each other.

Jim's father was proud that he had made a commit-
ment to take his son to school each day so that they
could have some special time together away from the
rest of the family. He had been told that this would
be good for their relationship and ease some of the
conflict that they were having. When Jim was asked
about this time he said that his dad spent most of the
time on his mobile phone and driving and they didn't
talk about anything, so he couldn't see the point of it.
Father and son had totally different views and what
had been an admirable plan had not worked out.
Sadly, Jim's father had missed the point of the
special time.

The special time is for you to rebuild your relationship, to help your child feel special and feel that his needs
are recognised. If you are not used to praising your child,
it needs practice. It can feel false initially, but once you
learn to notice the good things then it becomes easier.

Learning how to play

Play is a vital part of children's lives as they grow up. It
provides an opportunity to try out new skills and ideas, to
imitate what they have seen, to work out their feelings,
and to learn how to make friends and be in a social group.
Playing with your toddler is also a very important part of
your role as a parent. He needs you to watch and learn

from, to check out what is safe, and for help when he cannot manage on his own.

It can be tempting to leave your child to play on his own while you get on with the list of jobs that needs to be done; but you will find that you are continually interrupted, that he needs help or that he will come and play under your feet in order to maintain contact with you. Do take the opportunity when it is presented to find the time to play with your child every day. You may have forgotten how to play if this is your first child, so sit and watch and gradually build up confidence as your child involves you in his activity.

Play is a time for learning, but try not always to turn it into teaching. I have seen so many parents sit down to play with their children only to fire a set of questions at them. 'What colour is the car?' 'How many cars are there?' 'Let's count the cars.' 'What's this called?' 'What colour is her dress?' Your child wants to play not answer questions which are irrelevant, in his eyes, to the play.

It is also very easy to take over the play if you are not used to playing with preschoolers. You might be tempted to sort and categorise by putting all of the red cars together when all your child wants to do is push them around the floor making 'brum brum' noises. You might take over the Playdoh after initially showing him how to roll it out, but then you find that you are doing it rather than him. You start dressing all of the dolls while your child is busy undressing them all. Listen to yourself saying, 'I'll show you how to do it.' 'No, it goes like this.' 'That doesn't go there.' Be careful about how you play and try to watch your child; reflect what he is doing and be responsive to his approaches to you. Sometimes it is easy to involve yourself in play so much that you forget what your child is playing. You find that you do not want him to play with the train while you are putting it all together, because you want to play with it. If you find that your child tends to wander off or plays with something else while you are playing with him then think about what you are doing and whether he is being included in the play (Webster-Stratton & Herbert, 1994).

If you are having problems with managing your preschooler then play is an excellent way of fostering his positive side, increasing his cooperation to do as he is told, and improving your relationship. Sometimes it can feel worrying if all your preschooler wants to do is play aggressive games. Every time he picks up a toy he starts to shoot you with it, or hit toys together in a fight. You can feel very unsure how best to manage this.

Andy, a 4-year-old, worried his mother with the amount of anger and fighting he showed when playing with his toys. He had some animals and would always make the lion eat the others, and talked about legs and heads coming off and blood on the floor. He was obsessed with guns and would turn anything into a gun often pushing it into her face and shooting her. He would throw soft toys on the floor and jump on them angrily as if trying to destroy them.

Playing with a child who is showing a lot of aggressive play can feel upsetting. Research watching mothers playing with their aggressive children found that they tended to make value judgements about the play: '*Oh, that's a horrible thing to do*', '*That's not very nice*'. They often tried to stop the play by removing the toy or changing the topic of the game, or left the child alone when they played aggressively (Landy & Menna, 2001). But mothers of unaggressive children were more likely to join in the play, even if it was aggressive, by taking a role or talking for a toy. They were able to reflect their child's feelings and help damp down the aggression by keeping the child's feelings under control.

Saying how your child or the toy characters must be feeling is one way of stating out loud what is happening: '*I think he must feel very sad*', '*I bet he feels cross*'. Most children show some aggression in their play so, rather than trying to stop it because it worries you, it seems far better to allow your child to carry on as long as it doesn't accelerate into physical hitting or swearing. He may need help to calm down a bit if he is getting over-excited, so both you and he need to know the limits. If you join in the play and become one of the characters you are in a better position to be able to modulate what is happening. You will be able to talk about the character's feelings and keep the fantasy play safe. If a repetitive or destructive element keeps occurring, then you can elaborate the theme of the game by introducing new characters into the game or expanding the time frame. You can also introduce more social and cooperative themes while still playing within the fantasy structure that your child has established.

'*The lion would like to be friends with the rabbit now.*'

'*It is time for them to have supper together now? What would they like to eat?*'

'*The soldier has killed all of the animals, what is he going to do now? Do you think he could go in the truck and take all of those bags to the fort?*'

Play can help your child work out his anger and frustration but it should not be allowed to escalate out of control or become so repetitive that your child's play becomes restricted and unable to develop. Your child needs to use play to learn how to understand the views of others, to be sociable and cooperative and to be able to control how he feels. Gently moving him on when he gets stuck, by positive guidance rather than restricting what he is doing, is by far your best approach.

Sharon found that her 3-year-old, Sally, repetitively played doctors and nurses with her dolls on her own, going through the same procedure of giving her doll an injection and then putting her to bed. Sharon joined in and found that her daughter became more settled and accepting of her playing with her and began to talk more to her mother while telling her what to do in the game. They became more relaxed together and Sally started to sit on her mother's lap during the game and let her mother dress her dolls.

Supporting growth and exploration

There can be a tremendous sense of enjoyment and excitement at watching your child grow and develop. You learn rapidly that your child is not a blank slate on which you write your hopes and wishes for the future. He is an individual with his own needs to grow and learn, to investigate and explore. He wants to absorb the experiences of the world and needs you to modulate, protect and help him cope with what happens. He is learning at an enormous rate but thinks very differently to you. Many parents say, 'It will be easier when he can talk and I can reason with him', but in truth, if your child wants to do what he wants to do, no amount of reasoning will stop him. So don't live in false hopes that it will become easier. He still won't listen to you. You are up against willpower and a heady sense of success and power when he gets his own way.

Tina's mother was furious when her 2-year-old daughter had taken her lipsticks out of her cosmetic bag and then, after drawing on her own face with them had proceeded to draw on the new bed cover.

What do you think Tina was doing? Was she deliberately being naughty and determined to upset her mother? I guess from Tina's point of view she had seen her mother put on lipstick and wanted to do the same but lost the plot and started to experiment with a new drawing medium. She probably felt proud of her artwork and was surprised and confused when her mother was so cross. Should she have known better at age two?

Tom, aged three, narrowly avoided being seriously hurt after he had climbed on top of the wardrobe in his room and it had fallen over smashing into the chest of drawers, gouging a huge hole in the wall and destroying two pieces of furniture.

What was Tom doing? Was he being naughty or trying out his physical skills? Could he have anticipated that the wardrobe would fall over? He created a lot of expense for his parents who then felt he could not be trusted. They were furious with him but were they more concerned about the expense, about the possibility of him having injured himself or about his having been stupid? Do you think the parents stopped to analyse why they were angry? What do you feel Tom understood from his parents shouting at him? He was already frightened, shocked and upset. How could the parents react to help him understand the danger he had been in?

Exploring and testing the environment is a major way of learning for children. At times they make mistakes and get into trouble; but it is one way of them understanding the rules and expectations of our complex adult world. How many times have you been angry because your child's 'exploration' went wrong? Is this anyone's fault? As parents we learn by trial and error not to leave out the felt-tip pens when we are not around so that the wallpaper is not used as a drawing pad. We learn to move the TV out of reach of little fingers so that the exciting lesson of cause and effect is not learned by our 2-year-old turning the TV on and off repeatedly. We learn to put locks on the kitchen cupboards so that all of the pots and pans are not spread all over the floor. Hopefully, as experienced and intelligent adults, we learn to anticipate events so that catastrophes are avoided. But do we? Do we in fact become reactors to our child's behaviour, waiting for them to do something which we then try to stop? Sometimes our children grow up faster than we realise and they have moved onto the next stage of exploration while we are still coping with the earlier stage.

We want to encourage our children to be investigative, ask questions and understand what happens around them as it's a sign of intelligence. But we want them to investigate on our terms and within our rules. If they are not allowed to pick up grandma's ornaments from her low shelf, would you say, 'Don't do that, you'll drop them and break them', or would you say, 'Be careful, use two hands and then put it down gently. Shall I help you?' There is a big difference between these two approaches. One polices the behaviour and tries to stop it while blaming the child and anticipating a problem. The other helps the child explore safely with positive instructions about how to be careful. The offer of help is to alleviate your own sense of anxiety without upsetting the child. In one instance the child has learned how not to behave, i.e. if he touches then he will drop and break it; while in the other instance the child has learned a coping strategy, i.e. to use two hands and replace it gently. When this child goes to grandma's again which approach do you think will stop him touching the ornaments again, the one that stopped him and thwarted his exploration, or the one that satisfied his exploratory desire?

Another big difference in these approaches is the involvement of the parent. In the first solution the parent can shout from a distance and need not move unless the child does not obey, whereas in the second solution the parent is far more involved in thinking about how best to help the child in that situation. Problem-solving takes place and the parent has worked out what is a safe way for the child to explore. Usually a parent in this situation will go over to the child to prevent a disaster and help or show him how to hold it safely.

Lastly, I wonder which situation has the most potential for an escalation of reprimanding the child? Tempers build far more easily and rapidly when an instruction is ignored. Telling a child to stop doing something tends to leave a gap when the child has nothing to do, but saying a positive statement to the child about how to do it, or perhaps to do something else, fills the gap and directs the child into an acceptable behaviour.

Distracting your child

Many young children have difficulty redirecting their attention when it has been caught by something. They often repeat a behaviour and may even escalate it in order to increase their level of satisfaction, to gain attention or just to test the limits of what they are playing with.

Timmy, aged 12 months, was sitting on the floor playing with some wooden balls when he started to roll them along the floor until they hit the cupboard. It made a gratifying clonk and so he repeated it and after a few more times started to throw the ball at the cupboard to get a louder noise. His mother told him several times to stop but he continued. She eventually shouted at him and took away the balls so he cried and screamed in a temper tantrum.

What would have happened if his mother had offered him something else to play with, instead of the balls, which would not create so much noise or potential damage?

Marie was upset because her 2-year-old, Suzie, kept hitting her in the chest. Marie was worried that she had lost her temper and hit Suzie back on several occasions in an attempt to get her to stop. On watching mother and toddler play together it was clear they had a good relationship and enjoyed the play. After a quarter of an hour of playing with some puzzles, Suzie reached out and gently knocked her mother on the chest. Marie who was very conscious of this action immediately told her to stop and went back to playing with the puzzles again. Suzie then did it again slightly harder and Marie told her loudly to stop and pushed her hand away. Suzie immediately did it again harder and Marie started to shout and hit her hand away. When I intervened and offered Suzie another toy to play with she was immediately distracted and stopped hitting her mother.

It seemed that, although Marie could play well with Suzie, she was not anticipating that Suzie might get bored with the activity. So Suzie was tending to amuse herself by changing the activity and starting a new game of hitting. Marie then responded to the hit rather than directing Suzie's attention away onto something new to

do. Their interaction rapidly spiralled, as her
mother could not change the focus of attention.

Trying to stay one step ahead of your child is a very
valuable ability. Anticipating when he is likely to get
bored, understanding his short attention-span and watching for situations where problems are likely to occur is a
skill that can be practised and learned. When your child is
starting to lose his concentration, is starting to get bored
or is restricted in what he is allowed to touch then a change
of activity and interest is needed to prevent an escalation
into whining, demanding, crying or doing something that
perhaps you do not want him to do. Some children will
manage their own level of arousal by putting in their
thumb and having a quiet suck and will withdraw from
the world for a bit; but others who do not use this type of
self-calming or self-distracting activity will need you to
manage their feelings for them. To some parents it comes
naturally, but others find that thinking about their child
all of the time is too distracting from their own thoughts or
activities. Just think of the last time you went out shopping with your toddler in the buggy. How long did it take
before he started to get fractious and begin to want to get
out and do something else because he was fed up with you
looking at clothes and there was nothing he wanted to see?
What did you do?

- Did you tell him to be quiet and not make a fuss?
- Did you tell him that you would not be long?
- Did you offer him something to eat, drink or do?
- Did you promise that you would go to the toyshop
  next?
- Did you chat to him and engage him in what you
  were doing?

● Did you threaten to smack him if he carried on crying?

Preventing behaviour problems

Prevention is better than cure, so it seems far better to learn how to prevent children's behaviour problems than learn what do to once you have a problem. Prevention has two significant parts:

● learning to anticipate your children's behaviour;
● working out how to avoid the potential problem.

Anticipation involves learning about your child's behaviour by watching him. See how he plays and how long he lasts with any toy. What attracts him to touch and play with things? Are they noisy? Are they new? Does he need your help and guidance to help him play? Does he get frustrated with his own inability to do something? Does he try to break things and take them apart? How quickly does he get bored? Watch how he reacts in various situations: the supermarket, someone else's house. Once you know how your child behaves then you can start to anticipate what is going to happen and you will be prepared.

Anticipation is also helped by monitoring your preschooler all of the time. If he is out of your sight for ten minutes then he is likely to be exploring and is probably getting himself into trouble. Tina and Tim, the two children we mentioned at the beginning of this chapter, managed to get into trouble because their parent was not present and checking on what they were doing. It is a fact of life that you can no longer go and have a bath, or even go to the toilet, without knowing where your toddler is and what he is doing – and he may even be in there with you. One of the most noticeable features of families where children have the most difficult behaviour problems is the common lack of monitoring of the children (Patterson, 1982). So do keep an eye on your toddler all of the time. If you can't watch him, then make sure that your partner knows that they are carrying the responsibility for watching him. It really can be very tiring, because you feel that you have to have eyes in the back of your head and you never feel that you can totally concentrate on anything. It is why having your first child can be so tiring, because when you have more than one the older child will often report to you if the toddler is doing something that he shouldn't.

To avoid problems, use the knowledge that you have gained by watching your child and understanding his stage of development. Make the home environment safe, remove plants and electrical equipment off the floor once your baby is crawling. Use stair gates to prevent him going up and down stairs when you are not looking. Put child-proof locks on kitchen cupboards. When you are out of the home, have toys and food and drinks to use as distractions if your child is getting bored sitting in the buggy. Talk to him to involve him in your activities; sing songs to engage him and keep him happy. Go to the supermarket checkout that doesn't display sweets. Keep shopping trips short and don't expect him to sit happily for an hour in the buggy while you look at dresses.

There is an old study, a favourite of mine, that watched mothers with their preschoolers in supermarkets (Holden, 1983). It showed that mothers fell into three different types. Some mothers would shout at their children and tell them off when they started to misbehave. Another group would distract their children once they started to be difficult. While another group would avoid problems by talking to their children and involving them in the shopping. The mothers who were able to anticipate the problems and avoid them before they even started had the least problem. But the mothers who shouted had the greatest difficulty and their children made the greatest number of demands on them.

This study helps us recognise how parental behaviour has a marked impact on how children behave. Their learning is rapid and your child will be fully aware that you have something in your bag for him if that is a technique of distraction that you have used before. He will shout and demand sweets and crisps if you have quietened him with those previously. He will run off if he thinks he can get you to chase him and have a game. But if you see shopping as more of a joint activity in which your child participates, rather than sitting quietly while you get on, you will find that he will stay calmer for longer. Of course eventually he will get bored as he doesn't want to look at the things that you want to look at; but you can buy yourself some time without whingeing and crying.

This is a strong positive parenting method as it creates a positive relationship between you and your child. You are thinking of your child's needs and interests while also doing what you want to do. He feels involved and enjoys the attention and chat. He learns to observe things in his environment. You can guide his attention, expand his vocabulary and provide learning experiences. For example, encouraging him to help put the fruit and vegetables into the bags in the supermarket results in him touching and feeling these foods. He learns their names, their feel and their smell. He even learns to count. Chatting like this can be hard work and you sometimes feel a complete fool when you've spoken toddler-talk most of the day and carry on with it to your partner when he comes home.

This may be one important difference between men

and women as women in general do find it easier to chat about what they are doing, rather like giving a running commentary on their activities and thoughts, while men tend to be silent and not verbalise their thoughts to the same extent. So take advantage of it as your toddler will only benefit.

Coping with questions

Part of your child's drive to explore the world will result in him asking incessant questions once he is old enough. This can at times drive you to distraction. But generally children tend to only ask over and over again if they have not understood the answer, so be careful about how you explain and you will find the rate of question-asking reduces as he is satisfied. Keep your answers simple and within his ability to understand what you are saying. Don't fall into the trap of starting on a complex answer when a simple one will do.

David, aged 4 years, asked his father where rain came from one day while they were out walking. David's father then launched into a long discussion about water from the earth evaporating and then condensing in the sky where the temperature was lower. David kept asking, 'Why does it do that', until his father started to become exasperated. His mother interrupted with a brief statement, 'it comes from the clouds', which fully satisfied his enquiry.

Noticing good behaviour

It seems sad that we seem to be attuned to noticing problems and bad things that happen. Only bad news is news.
It is often the case that we ignore our children when they
are being quiet or behaving well but suddenly say something to them if they start to misbehave or be noisy.
Nearly all of their good behaviour is not commented on
but their bad behaviour gets quite a strong reaction.
This is partly to do with our methods of learning. We
need regular and positive feedback when we are
learning a new skill so that we can adjust what we are
doing to be more accurate. But once we have learned the
skill we don't need that high level of feedback, a positive
comment every now and again is enough to keep us online.
If we are being the teacher we automatically expect our
learner not to need such frequent feedback once they
know how to do a task. This 'intermittent' or irregular
feedback is usually sufficient to keep the learner happy.
No wonder I hear parents say, 'He ought to know how to
behave!', 'Why should I tell him he's being good, he
knows that he should be?' We assume that once our children have been taught to be good that they should
continue to be so.

But if you remember back to your schooldays or your
own childhood, you may well have very clear memories of
teachers that you liked, who encouraged you and told you
when you were doing well, and teachers who were critical
and always seemed to pick out your bad points and made
you feel unhappy. I am not saying that we should never
criticise children or point out a problem that needs cor-
recting, as this is part of learning, but they also need the
positive feedback to keep up their self-esteem and to be
reminded about how well they are doing. The criticism

without the praise can lead to poor motivation, fear, anxiety, avoidance and defiant behaviour.

Young children are very dependent on attention from their parents and will seek it out if it is not being offered. So it is easy to see that if they don't get attention for good behaviour they will rapidly find out that they can get attention for bad behaviour and therefore that will start to increase. You can see, therefore, the importance of giving your child positive feedback and praise when he is playing quietly or constructively, has sat well at the table, has eaten his meal, has come when you called or has done what you have asked. You are encouraging him and reminding him of how to behave well, not just expecting him to do it.

So positive comments, praise, pats, strokes, hugs, telling your partner in front of your child about how helpful he has been are all important ways of keeping the good times rolling. Focusing on the good and trying to ignore the bad will change your focus and help you and your child develop a more positive relationship.

Increasing your child's self-confidence and self-esteem

Ideally we would like our children to grow up feeling good about themselves, being able to cope with their own feelings and being able to empathise with others' feelings. We live in a competitive world and some parents may consider that emotional sensitivity is the opposite of the aggressively competitive skills needed to succeed. But it is not always possible to be top of the pile and we mostly have to cope with being some way down but feel OK about it. I always remember a Charlie Brown cartoon of many years ago when Charlie entered a spelling competition at school and he did really well and managed to get into the finals. Sadly he lost on the final round by one point and was totally dejected and felt a complete failure. He had not appreciated that he had tried his best and had done exceedingly well even though he had not come top.

Helping children feel good about themselves is one way of inoculating them against bumps they will have throughout their lives. We are not all geniuses and there will always be someone who finds the work easier or gets better marks at school. To avoid giving up the competition and saying it's all a waste of time we need to help our children feel good about their achievements and their efforts. Most schools now have 'Effort' grades on school reports, and those are really more important than the 'Achievement' grade. Children with low self-esteem tend to think that things are too hard for them to do. They avoid challenging themselves as they think they will fail. They may feel worried or anxious and are easily discouraged. They may then seek lots of reassurance, take ages to get going on anything, be very hesitant and repeatedly need encouragement.

Self-esteem and self-confidence start in the preschool years. A child whose efforts at art are laughed at or turned upside-down and asked, 'What is it?', will feel embarrassed and start to hide their work, tear it up, say 'it's no good' or stop doing it. Putting your child's artistic effort on the fridge, encouraging him to talk about what he has done in the picture, pointing out good bits and saying what a good painter he is will produce a totally different set of feelings in him. He is more likely to try again, improve his efforts and be proud to show you what he had done.

Your warmth and care as a parent are the most significant features of developing good self-esteem in your children. Your continuous and close attachment is a vital building block for how they perceive themselves and how they value themselves. Your value of them is reflected in how they grow to value themselves. Think of friends that you know and how they talk about their childhoods and how their parents treated them. Many adults will describe how their parents had high standards that they could never reach. They never felt that what they achieved was good enough. Sometimes that criticism is internalised and comes out again when they are parents and they suddenly find themselves creating the same demands for their children.

Jack, aged 5 years, was lying continually at home and at nursery. He made up complex stories about how his father had a new car, that he had a special new toy at home, that his cat had been run over and a number of other smaller everyday lies. His parents were very worried and had tried a number of punishments none of which had any long-term effect. His father was a very strict and critical man who felt that Jack needed to be toughened up to face the world. He did not believe in saying something was good if he didn't think that it was, and tended to treat his son as he did his subordinates at work. He had very high standards and found it difficult to praise his son. Jack had become very anxious and lacked self-confidence to the point that he was making up stories to make himself seem important with his friends and at nursery.

Siblings can also have a significant impact on a child's self-confidence. A younger child may be always trying to be like the elder one. Your children will have different strengths and weaknesses and if one is good at football while the other isn't this can lead to a lot of resentment and avoidance of even trying because of the innate competition between siblings. One may be more musical, more artistic or more academic than the other. It is up to you to help bring out their strengths and help them feel that their efforts are worth it. In general it is probably easier to help them shine at different activities. If you are a musical family then encourage different instruments, if you are a sporty family encourage different sports to suit each child's temperament and abilities.

The other main element in developing a sense of self-esteem is how you define your child to himself. Over-generalising when reprimanding a child will attribute bad characteristics that can stick.

- 'You never listen to what I say.'
- 'You are always such a naughty boy.'
- 'You've got a bad memory.'
- 'You are a very rude and bad-tempered girl.'

These statements are over-inclusive and make a personality feature out of an event. As parents we have to remember to list the event or behaviour as a problem, not the child.

- 'I don't like it when you lose your temper, because you can be so helpful at other times.'
- 'I feel unhappy when you are rude to your brother.'

I guess the opposite is not such a problem. It is nice to

receive an over-generalisation of a good behaviour: 'You are so musical', 'You are so beautiful.' But we need to be careful that the standard set is not too high and out of keeping with how the child feels. It is much safer to keep evaluative comments to specific instances and then you don't run the risk of imposing your evaluation of a good quality of the child upon them. It is safer to say, 'That's a great picture, you have painted it so well', rather than, 'You are such a good artist'. Once you learn to praise the action of your child you find that it applies in all sorts of situations that have nothing to do with your generalisation of him as 'good' or 'bad'. You can praise him for each little instance of behaviour even though you may feel that generally he doesn't listen or is too active. Being specific helps you focus on details of what happens and notice the good points, and avoids the tendency to only notice the bad.

The over-protective parent is the other obstacle for a child's self-esteem and self-confidence to battle against. If you are a worrier and are overly concerned about your child's safety and so resist him taking risks of any sort you could be interfering with your child's natural ability to explore and find out his own strengths and weaknesses. Over-generalisations, like a worried, 'Be careful', increases your child's worry rather than helping him to take more care. 'Do you want to hold my hand as you walk on the wall?' is more constructive and identifies to your child that you are available to help if he gets into a problem. Doing things for your child rather than encouraging self-reliance and coping skills will make your child more dependent and he will not realise that he can manage on his own. As your toddler grows he will want to be more independent. Your job is to help him through safe transitions so that he learns to manage by himself, become more self-reliant and confident. You need to let him go a little in order for him to develop and learn.

Suzie, aged 4 years, would cry about doing PE at nursery as she could not do up her buttons. Her mother had always dressed her in the morning and had never taught her how to dress herself. She was very close to her mother and felt anxious when her mother was not around. Mrs D. had to be encouraged to help Suzie learn self-help skills rather than do everything for her.

We all gain confidence by practice and doing. If we don't try we never learn and never face up to the problems that we fear. We all make mistakes but they are not the end of the world and we can often learn from them. So encourage your child to experiment and try new activities, to deal with change and to be flexible enough to cope with what life throws at him.

Stimulating creativity

Creativity is the ability to show original thought, to be inventive and to show imagination. Children are not bound with the limitations of structured learning approaches that govern adult thought much of the time, and it is often easy to see their creativity become swamped by having to stick to rules or boundaries that we set. We do like the paint on the paper and not on the carpet. We do like the sand in the sand pit and not on the lawn. How do we stimulate and foster creative ideas but still maintain the boundaries that we need to keep for our own sanity?

We are all guilty of focusing children's answers to the 'correct' one. When we are in teaching mode we tend to ask closed questions. 'What colour is the bus?', 'How many shoes do you have?', rather than open questions, 'I wonder how many different coloured buses we can find?' This could stimulate a day-long search or discussion with friends about all of the different colours of buses they have seen. At nursery and school, children are often taught the 'right' answers and the 'right' way of working out the problem. But research work has shown that 3- and 4-year-olds can generate many different solutions to solving problems that stimulates their ability to think and be creative (Shure & Spivak, 1978). Encouraging your child to think of as many different solutions to a problem as possible will help him generate ideas and foster his creative thinking. 'I wonder how many ways we can think of getting those toys into the box?' Your child will do it backwards, through his legs, upside-down, with his left hand, with his foot – and suddenly you have the floor cleared.

Children's ideas and solutions can be magical, totally unrealistic or outside the bounds of natural law, because they don't know about natural law. The magical thoughts are the most fascinating. No wonder Harry Potter has caught on so rapidly! Sadly, we often correct imaginative ideas as wrong: 'That dog can't have pink hair it should be brown'. 'Elephants can't fly.' Beware that your own lack of imagination does not stultify your child's.

If you see your child repeating the same picture over and over again, consider how to extend his thinking. 'I wonder how many different colours that dress could be?', 'I wonder how many different shapes of windows that house could have?', 'I bet that tank could have more than one gun.' Your child may be repeating a formula that he knows gains praise and is easy to do. He has stopped thinking and creating.

Helping your child to make friends

Stimulating your child to think is an essential part of him learning to problem-solve in all sorts of ways. An aggressive child is one who has a limited range of ways of responding to social problems. If he wants a toy he grabs it and pushes the other child away. If you ask him what else he could do to get the toy he will think of hitting, kicking and shoving but these are all aggressive ways of behaving and are not very different in the effect they have on others. These children have a problem in generating ideas that are not aggressive and end up not having any friends. They need to learn that there are other solutions to the problem of getting the toy that they want.

- Waiting until the other child has finished playing with the toy.
- Bargaining or offering a swop with another toy.
- Asking the teacher or parent to help in getting the toy.
- Joining in play with the child who is playing with the toy.

If your child is being predominantly aggressive with other children, then he is probably getting stuck in one style of response. Sadly, it is often successful as other children will give in, in order not to be hurt, so your child is encouraged to carry on being aggressive to get his own way, unless an adult intervenes. Sometimes other children will cry and complain about what has happened, which brings the behaviour to the attention of adults, and then they start to reject playing with the aggressive child and will not allow him to join in their games. This social isolation adds to the problem as the aggressive child no longer has a way of learning from watching others how best to negotiate conflicts. He resorts back to the method he knows best, which is aggression.

How do you break out of this cycle? Your child seems to attract negative attention. He is always being told off, he is always in trouble and he doesn't seem to learn. He will bully other children to play with him and usually the play time will end up in crying or a fight. If you talk about the problem with him he will always blame the other child and never see his role in the conflict.

He needs to learn how to think through and solve the problem creatively and work out what the consequences are of behaving in different ways. This may sound very hard for a 4-year-old; but he can be taught this. It can be helpful for you to apply this to yourself and think through what you might say or do if you had an argument with your partner. If you can work out ways in which both of you end up happy, you are starting to think about positive ways of solving the conflict and also have the goal of a positive solution. When we argue we are usually busy trying to put our own point of view across and denying the other person the right to say or do anything differently. We may even want to hurt them emotionally because we feel hurt. We don't often think of a positive goal. I guess your child feels much the same. He is so concerned with what he wants he does not think of the consequences or the other child's feelings, he is only thinking of getting his own way.

We have a tendency to short-cut learning and tell our children how we want them to behave, but don't help them sort it out for themselves. Often the lessons are not heard. Think how differently you feel when your mother tells you how to manage your child and when your friend tries to help you work out what is the best approach for you. Who do you listen to? How do you learn best?

Siblings are fighting over a train.

Mum: *Stop fighting and be quiet.*

Tim: *It's mine, I want it. Mum he won't give it to me.*

Sam: *Go away, I'm playing with it.*

Mum: *Will you two stop arguing?*

Argument continues.

Mum: *I'll take it away from both of you, unless you stop fighting.*

Has this mother helped either child resolve the problem? She has stated what she wants to happen and what she is going to do, but she has not helped the problem solving. If she is going to interfere then she needs to consider what her children need to learn in order to play together. Another dialogue could be:

Mum: *Why are you two fighting and making such a noise?*

Tim: *He's got my train and I want it.*

Mum: *Sam, why won't you give it to Tim?*

Sam: *He's been playing with it for ages and I want a go.*

Mum: *Tim, what else would you like to play with, while Sam has a go with the train?*

Tim: *Nothing, I want the train.*

Mum: *OK, you two, you tell me how we work this out. You both want to play with the train but there is only one train. What can you do?*

This does not solve the problem for the boys but poses it and asks them to think of solutions. The solution they arrive at may not be what you want, e.g. Sam may just give it up; but it is a solution and they have thought about how to work out the problem. They will then be able to think better the next time about a fairer way of sharing.

If your child hits another child you can ask why he did it and what the other child said or did and whether his reaction was a good idea or not. He can be reminded that hitting is just one thing that he can do and then he can be asked if he can think of something different that will solve the problem (Shure & Spivak, 1978). Part of this process is heightening his awareness of how others feel and how they feel similar or different to him at the same time.

'How did John feel when you hit him?'

'He cried.'

'Do you think he felt happy about it?'

'*No, he was unhappy.*'

'*How were you feeling?*'

'*I was cross.*'

'*So you both were feeling unhappy at the end. Was that a good way to end it?*'

'*No*'

'*What else could you have done to make it end better?*'

Working through problems and conflicts with your child will help him realise that there are other ways he can behave. The focus is on how he thinks, not necessarily on the solutions that he comes to at the time. Try not to evaluate his solutions for him, but encourage him to think about what will happen if he does what he says so that he learns to anticipate and work out the consequences for himself.

Children are rejected by their peers when they do not show sociable behaviour (Denham *et al.*, 1990). It is not just being aggressive that is the problem. We have assumed that sociable behaviour is something that children learn as they get older, how to control their feelings and become aware of other people's feelings; but this does start in the preschool years.

Encouraging sharing and turn-taking

Sharing and turn-taking are very different abilities. The tendency to offer or give objects to others is evident around 8 months of age (Hay *et al.*, 1999). Young toddlers will readily feed their siblings or friends from their own spoon and plate. But during their third year of life they start to become aware of possessions particularly their own. At first this may seem funny when he won't share his sweets but possessively hugs the bag. Left unchecked it can cause some problems. So it seems that our children are able to share at a younger age and then seem to lose this ability and have to relearn it. They make a developmental shift in awareness about possessions, become consciously aware of choice and develop preferences for what they want.

Encouraging sharing is something that you can do on a daily basis, by doing it yourself and showing your child how to share. You can prompt him to do it and praise him when he complies so that he realises it is important to do. One of the many vital roles that a parent has to play is to teach their child to share. It is the basis of social living and is essential if a child is to survive school. Sharing is a naturally taught skill. Think how often you have shared some food from your plate with your toddler. You have continual opportunities to teach sharing, e.g. sharing out sweets between your children rather than giving them their own bag, or asking your toddler to offer a crisp from his bag to every one in the family. We sometimes feel that it is easier to get each child their own toys and possessions so that the number of squabbles are reduced; but at times it is important to think about teaching them to share a set of crayons, to share time on the computer, to share some paper and paints.

Mrs S. had started to despair of her daughter's behaviour, as Mary, aged two, would have a

tantrum any time a friend came to play at her house.
She was fine when she went to play at other friends'
houses but the problem occurred only in her house
and her mother felt embarrassed that she could not
invite anyone back. Mary was very possessive of her
own toys and would not let her friends play with
anything of hers, but was only too happy to play
with their toys.

We discussed how her mother should help her
learn to share. Mrs S. would remove Mary's
newest and favourite toys out of sight and would
leave out a few older toys that she was not so
attached to. With her mother's support and encouragement and controlled access to toys Mary
gradually learned to play better in her own home.

Sharing is an interesting skill as we find it far easier to
share with people we like rather than those we don't like,
so sharing is also a way of indicating approval and liking
for someone else. It also involves waiting until the other
person has finished with what you want to use. Self-
control and the ability to tolerate a time delay and a
sense of frustration are necessary.

Young children pass through an 'egocentric' phase
when they think that the whole world revolves around
them and their desires. They find it nearly impossible to
wait and have no real concept of taking turns. Learning to
wait is a skill that can be taught simply and in stages.
Helping your child wait for a short time initially is the
first step. Half a minute may be enough for a 2-year-old
and then he should be congratulated for waiting quietly.
You can build up the length of time gradually and in

keeping with your child's age and development. But always remember to give positive feedback for waiting patiently.

Problems arise when your child does not understand what you mean by, 'Wait a minute', when you are in the middle of washing up and he wants you to read him a story. Toddlers are designed to interrupt our activities and they have no concept that they are interrupting, they are only thinking about their needs. They will grab you around the legs or push you and hang onto your clothes in order to get what they want, continually whining and demanding. Your toddler has no idea what 'a minute' is and you actually don't mean that. It is far better to be realistic and say, 'When I've finished washing up I'll read you a story'. You can then ask him if he wants to stand on a chair to watch you finish what you are doing.

Many preschool board and card games involve taking turns with one another and these provide an excellent way in which you can teach your child on a one-to-one basis. Waiting for one other person to have a turn is often as much as he can manage initially, so don't launch into games that require four people playing.

Timmy was very difficult in playgroup. He would insist on going to the top of the slide and would push other children out of the way aggressively in order to get to the top. He was becoming a danger to others.

His mother, helped by the playgroup coordinator, planned to teach him to wait, at first by holding his hand in the queue while he waited behind one child, then letting him wait by himself behind one child and gradually increasing the number of children in the queue so that he could wait for longer periods. He was regularly praised for waiting without pushing and managed to learn this new skill within two attendances at the nursery.

Sue found that her 3-year-old daughter was becoming very difficult in shops. If she bought her something she would not let her mother give it to the shopkeeper to buy it. She would have a massive temper tantrum, throw herself on the floor and make such a scene that her mother did not want to buy the present for her any more. She did not seem to understand that she had to give the present to the shopkeeper first before she could have it back. It did not make sense to her as she just saw her present being moved out of sight.

Play can help learning in such a situation. Playing shops at home helped Sue teach her 3-year-old the sequence of events. She learned that, after choosing what she wants to buy, it has to be paid for and put in a bag before she can take it away.

Love and time

The old adage that 'they are grown up before you have fully enjoyed them' seems to ring hollow when you are in the midst of temper tantrums, sleepless nights and wet beds. But this is the time when you are at the centre of your child's world and he needs and loves you with his whole being. Take time to reflect on how his desire to be with you all of the time is not just an irritation but a reflection of how he needs you to help him cope with the world. He needs your protection and love. It may seem that you are giving all of the time, but if you watch and let yourself be open to your child, you will find how he cuddles up, likes to stroke your hair while sucking his thumb, how he shows you proudly what he has done. Look at him asleep and see how angelic he looks after the battles of the day. Think about all of the lovely little things that happen each day rather than the problems.

You may be stressed by all of the jobs that need to be done: you don't have any time and he seems to delay you and get in the way. Take a breather and reflect on whether you really need to do all of those jobs. The first 5 years of your child's life will never be repeated so try to have fun and enjoy him. He needs your time and your love to grow and develop. It can take great patience but the care that you take now will pay dividends later in his life.

Topical tips

- Focus on the good and try to ignore the bad.

- A special play time each day can improve your relationship with your child.

- Distracting young children can avoid a confrontation.

- Prevention is better than cure.

- Try to stay one step ahead of what your child is going to do next.

- Always know where your toddler is and what he is doing.

- Involve your child in what you are doing.

- Notice and comment on your child's good behaviour.

- Help your child feel good about himself and what he does.

- Valuing your child's efforts will increase his self-esteem.

- Encourage your children to find their own strengths.

- Criticise a behaviour not the whole child.

- Encourage your child to think of lots of different solutions to problems.

- Aggressive behaviour reflects a limited pattern of problem-solving.

- Encourage sharing and learning to wait for a turn.

3

Setting limits

We live, work and play in groups. Any group of people will tend to create a set of rules of behaviour that all members of the group learn. Imagine playing football without knowing the rules of the game. What would be the aim of the game? In which direction would you run? Who would you pass the ball to? Children create rules for their own games and sometimes change them as they go along, but they do understand about the need to communicate their thoughts about the rules to their friends so that the friends can join in.

As parents we have the job of teaching our children about the rules of the society in which we live. We have the task of teaching them right from wrong, respect for others' feelings, obedience, cooperation, and hundreds of other ways of living in groups. This is the task of socialisation: helping your child learn how to be sociable with others and live cooperatively with them. The most important part of this process is being able to put their own needs and wants aside and to comply with the

expectations of others. It is something that we all battle
with throughout our lives!

As your baby grows into a toddler you will find that
the strength of his personality will at times be overpowering. As a baby he has very clear demands that need to be
met immediately, but as he grows older you begin to
realise that he can learn to wait, that he should not have
the bar of chocolate he wants before his supper, that he
can't have all of the toys he wants from the shop. You start
to realise that you have to learn how to say 'no'.

How to say 'no'

It is interesting how hard we find it to say 'no' to our
children. Why should that be? Do we feel that saying
'no' is like withdrawing our love? Is saying 'no' creating
restrictions and building a cage? Is learning about 'no' the
loss of innocence? Are we worried that our children will
not love us if we say 'no'?

> *Sandy was completely worn out and exhausted with
> caring for her toddler. She was still breast-feeding
> her 2-year-old as she felt that Jade would give up
> the breast when she wanted to. Jade was still de-
> manding breast-feeding up to 20 times a day and
> her appetite was being affected. Jade preferred
> breast-feeding to eating and the range of foods that
> she would eat was limited so her weight was poor.
> The breast milk was not providing sufficient nutri-
> tion for a child of her age.*

In addition Sandy was getting very little sleep, as she had never succeeded in encouraging Jade to sleep on her own. She had taken her into her bed and had thought that Jade would leave to sleep in her own bed when she was ready. Consequently Jade was helping herself to breast-feeding several times during the night, which disturbed Sandy's sleep.

Sandy felt strongly that if she was always available to Jade that her daughter would eventually create the separation when she was ready. But meanwhile Sandy was being run into the ground, was feeling depressed, and was not taking care of herself. She desperately loved Jade and did not want to have to say 'no'. She wanted to be available to her daughter 24 hours a day, but had lost sight of her own needs as a person and of the fact that she needed to be well and to be able to cope in order to provide a safe and caring home for Jade.

Sandy's attitudes are not uncommon, and there are always parents who will report how effective this approach was for them and how their child gradually lost interest in the breast or managed to transfer to his own bed on his own without a battle. But they forget to mention that you need to be prepared to breast-feed occasionally until your child starts school, or have them in your bed until the age of 5 or 6 years. Sandy's aims were destroying her health and her emotional strength so it was important for her to review how best to progress and to feel that it was reasonable to set limits to Jade's behaviour in order to feel safe. She felt guilty that resentment was building up inside her and it was starting to destroy her feelings towards Jade.

One of the most common first restrictions that parents impose is around sleep. Many parents find that they say 'no' for the first time in relation to toddlers who won't go to sleep at bedtime and want more cuddles or stories. You know that your toddler needs to go to sleep or he will be irritable the next day, but he doesn't know this and so carries on demanding your attention. Should you give in and let him stay up to avoid a battle? Should you lie down with him and cuddle him until he falls asleep or is this creating a precedent? Should you say 'no' and set a clear signal to him that you are leaving him and that he should settle to sleep? It can feel painful to withdraw yourself from your child when he is asking for your company. No wonder we get into a muddle.

We are there to meet our children's needs and help them grow and develop but at what point do we start to teach them the rules? I feel horror when I see cars racing down the motorway with young children bouncing around in the back seats, not wearing seat belts. Maybe the children fought against having them on so the parents gave in; but what risks are those children being exposed to because their parents could not say 'no'? Do the parents feel that they are being kind letting the children have fun on the back seat? Or have they given up trying to control them, not knowing how to say 'no' as the children never listen to them? What has happened when a 3-year-old has more control in the family than the 30-year-old mother or father? What has happened when parents say their children are out of their control even before they have started school?

Setting limits for our children is a way of showing

them how to be safe, contained and loved. I have seen
many children who are in control of their parents but
who are unhappy, and seem to be ever more demanding
and insecure. Parents say, 'We give him everything and
yet he seems so unhappy and unsure'. These children are
often crying out for containment. They don't know
where the boundaries are and so continually push to
find out when their parents are going to contain them.
If you don't know where a boundary is, it is tempting
always to go a bit further to see what happens. Lack of
boundaries can make us feel unsure and insecure, as we
don't know what to expect. But you do need to realise
that you can say 'no' without always having a big argument and upset.

   There are many different ways of setting limits for
children, and you need to learn how to use the whole
range of techniques. Parents who are having problems
controlling their children may be giving in all of the
time and being trampled on, or they may be using
threats and punishments as their primary mode of
control. If I had 10 pounds for every time I had heard a
parent ask me how to find more effective punishments for
their children, I would be a rich woman. This seems so
sad and I am sure the parents don't realise how they have
got into this dreadful position. As adults we feel that
children should listen to what we say and do as they are
told. If they don't we start to try to make them by force.
We shout, we tell them off, we threaten to punish them
and then do punish them in order to get them to do what
we want. We act as policemen in terms of restricting
activity and making decisions. But over time we find
that this seems to work less well. Our children tend not
to care about the threats; they even pretend that the punishments don't bother them. Bravado sets in and the
parents feel helpless. This downward spiral can lead to
physical punishment and aggression in some households.

There are two main situations where we need to learn how to say 'no'. Firstly when you want to stop your child doing something, e.g. turning the TV on and off repeatedly; secondly when you are refusing to do what your child wants, e.g. not buying him sweets when he asks for them. If your child is being 'naughty' frequently and you find yourself shouting a lot, it is time to take stock and think about what is happening. You are probably finding that your shouting is not having much effect and that your child never seems to listen to you, let alone obey you.

You might ask yourself why is your child being so naughty?

- Is he trying to attract my attention?

- Is he trying to make me laugh?

- Is he just amusing himself?

- Is he exploring?

- Is he being creative?

- Is he distressed and angry?

- Is he jealous?

- Is he anxious or worried?

- Is he frustrated?

If you don't know the answer then start to analyse what is happening. But first you need to work what it is that you think is 'naughty'. Make a list during the day of what happens. Focus on the behaviour that makes you shout at him. This will help you think about how you want him to behave and what you want to change. From this list choose one behaviour that you want to change.

How he is	How I want him to be
Refuses to put his toys away at bedtime	Put his toys away when asked
Refuses to get dressed in the morning when I ask him	Get dressed when I ask him
Takes his sister's toys	Play cooperatively with his sister
Fights being put in the car seat	Accept being put in the car seat with no fuss
Screams at the checkout in the supermarket	Sit quietly at the checkout in the supermarket

The second task is to think about one behaviour and try to understand the sequence of events that often occurs and how your reactions may or may not change his behaviour.

- What starts the problem? It often involves you expecting him do what you want, but it can equally involve you refusing to do what he wants. If you think of this as 'making a demand' it can start with you, or him or another member of the family.
- What is your response? Do you give in? Do you stay calm and say 'no'? Or do you shout at him to make him cooperate?

- What effect does your response have? Does he carry on and ignore you? Does he run away? Does he shout back. Does he cry?
- What happens next?

It can be helpful to put this into a chart on a daily basis to see the pattern. These are called ABC charts as they record the Antecedents (the trigger), the Behaviour (the problem) and the Consequences (what you did in response).

Antecedents	Behaviour	Consequence
Tom sees sweets at checkout in supermarket	Tom cries and shouts for sweets to be given to him	I buy them to keep him quiet
Tom is playing with his sister and she takes his truck	Tom yells at Mary, pulls her hair, pushes her over and grabs the truck back	Mary starts screaming. I told off Tom for hurting his sister
I said it was time for bed and asked Tom to put the toys away in the box	Tom ran away and started throwing toys around and refused to do what I asked	I shouted at him to help and then started picking up the toys myself

Sometimes your response to the problem sets up the next problem. In the first example in the table, what do you think will happen the next time Tom and his parent go to the supermarket and he sees the sweets? In the second example, what has Mary learned from this experience? Has Tom learned to put away his toys when asked?

A research study in the USA showed how a cycle of unpleasant interaction could build up between parent and child (Patterson, 1982). It is surprising how quickly refusing a child's or a parent's demand can spiral into anger and sometimes aggression.

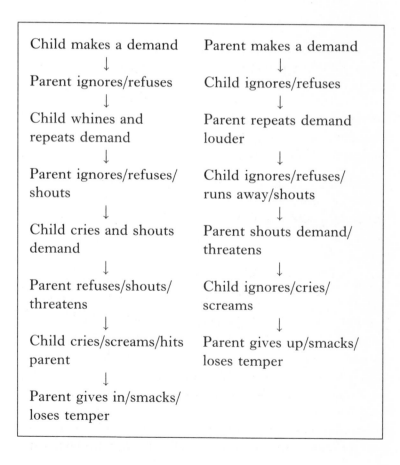

Child makes a demand	Parent makes a demand
↓	↓
Parent ignores/refuses	Child ignores/refuses
↓	↓
Child whines and repeats demand	Parent repeats demand louder
↓	↓
Parent ignores/refuses/ shouts	Child ignores/refuses/ runs away/shouts
↓	↓
Child cries and shouts demand	Parent shouts demand/ threatens
↓	↓
Parent refuses/shouts/ threatens	Child ignores/cries/ screams
↓	↓
Child cries/screams/hits parent	Parent gives up/smacks/ loses temper
↓	
Parent gives in/smacks/ loses temper	

These are common illustrations of how rapidly a small issue can end up being a big issue. How often have you found yourself on this track? You may not have smacked your child, but you will probably have shouted at him and shown anger and irritation. Emotions have become all entangled with control issues. You feel exasperated because your child won't listen to you, then you feel anger at the continual pressure your child is exerting. You may end up losing your temper and the whole situation has ended up feeling unpleasant and unhappy. Who is the winner?

The problem is that this interaction ends up with both parent and child feeling unhappy and angry with each other. Often the parent then feels guilty and may give the child what he asked for. This spiral is so easy to fall into when you are feeling generally stressed, tired or unhappy for other reasons. Your temper is short and you don't have the patience to deal with the pressure from your child.

Why won't he listen to me?

Why doesn't your child realise a bit earlier in the spiral that it is pointless to continue asking for something that he cannot have? The reality is that parents are inherently inconsistent. We sometimes give in on the first asking, or it may take three or four attempts before we give in. It depends a bit on our mood and on what other things have happened that lead us to be more likely to say 'yes' or 'no'. Your child is busy trying to work out how to get his own way and so just tries harder because in the past you have sometimes given in.

Being inconsistent is one of the biggest problems we

have to face as parents. The reasons why we give in sometimes are not clear to the child and are bound up with our
own thoughts about how we want our children to be
happy, how we want them to have what they want (but
within limits), how we want them to have what we never
had, how we want to be reasonable. If our child really puts
on the pressure we may falter because of a difference in
attitude between the two parents, or because we realise
that our child really wants it so badly that it seems mean
to deprive them. The uncertainty in our response to our
children's demands is the basis for the continual pressure
and the apparent lack of acceptance of when we say 'no'.
So many parents say their child appears not to understand
what 'no' means. Could this be because 'no' has never
really meant 'no' but has meant 'well possibly, if you
push me hard enough'? If you want your child do what
you want, but don't expect him to do, or ensure that he
does do, as you ask, then you are just teaching him to
ignore you.

Your first golden rule of child management is to think
before you speak.

- What is my reason for saying 'no', or for wanting
  him to do what I want?
- Do I really mean it?
- Can I stick to my decision or request?
- Do I have time to stick to my decision or request?
- Is it an important enough issue for me to see it
  through to the end?

If you can't stick to your decision or request, then don't
say it in the first place. If you want your child to help clear
up the toys, you have to ensure that he does it with you
rather than you doing it once he has run off.

How can I be firm without losing my temper?

Being firm is necessary when you are trying to get your child to do something that he doesn't want to do. It is essential to stay calm and in control, you will be far more effective and think more clearly if you can keep your emotions well under control. Losing your temper is admitting defeat, and then you feel ashamed of yourself for not showing more self-control. How can you expect your child to control his temper if you cannot control yours?

It is far easier to stay in control if you feel confident about what you are doing. Knowing how to approach a problem is the key. If you have a plan, then you have a sense of direction and can anticipate what is going to happen. You should use a variety of different strategies rather than sticking to shouting and pressure. Standing back from the situation and being more objective can also help to separate you from the emotional surge. Count to 10 if you feel yourself getting angry, and talk yourself down. You are at your most vulnerable when you are feeling tired, stressed or ill, so beware of those times, give yourself some leeway and don't expect too much from your child.

Methods for stopping 'naughty' behaviour:

- Distraction works well with younger children who have not developed the memory skills to push through a strong desire. They are more responsive to what is happening in front of them and they can easily forget if provided with another interesting object or activity.

Stopping your child doing what he wants	Teaching your child to do what you want
Distract him	Clear simple instruction
Ignore him	Clear positive consequences for cooperation
Prevent him	Monitor cooperation
Tell him to stop	Reinforce all attempts to cooperate
Remove him (time out)	Physically and verbally prompt
Remove yourself	Use humour/challenge/competition
Offer incentives for stopping	
Tell him to carry on and do it more	

● Ignoring your child's provocative bad behaviour can sometimes make it disappear. If your child tends to do something while looking at you with a smile or checks that you are looking, he is doing it to get a reaction. If you decide not to react then you really must control yourself and not react even when he has done it for the fourth or fifth time or he will learn that he really has to try hard to annoy you. Turning the TV on and off gets boring after a while and your child will go away and do something else to amuse himself. But if it leads to a good

reaction from you and a game develops of you trying
to catch him to stop him doing it, then this will be a
great activity when he is bored. Withdrawal of your
attention is a very powerful tool and if your child
suspects that you are upset and not responding he
will feel more upset than if you shout at him.

- Prevention is better than cure in many instances
  with young children. Make sure that valuable or
  breakable objects are out of reach. Make sure that
  the environment at home is safe. Go to the checkout
  that doesn't have the sweets on display. Keep drinks
  and food in the kitchen so that they are not spread
  all over the carpet. Lock cupboards that contain
  precious or dangerous items. Use stair gates.

- Tell him to stop so that he knows what you want. Be
  clear that you will make him stop if he carries on.
  Don't just nag and nag repeatedly, or shout across
  the room at him. Get up and either move him, take
  the object away or physically stop him from what he
  is doing. If you need to say 'no' then do, but stick
  with it.

- Removing him from the situation will avoid further
  problems. Take him to another room so that he is
  not tempted to carry on. 'Time out' involves removing your child from what he is doing and making
  him sit down on a cushion or a chair for a few
  minutes to calm down. At times removing yourself
  from the situation is the best solution, particularly if
  you feel you are going to lose your temper.

- Providing rewards and incentives for good behaviour
  is probably the most useful way of encouraging your
  child to behave better. You are saying what you
  want in a positive manner and providing him with
  the choice of whether he earns the reward by complying.

- Telling him to carry on and do it more is a paradoxical way of stopping bad behaviour, but can be quite risky.

Methods for encouraging cooperation:

- Clear, simple instructions. Preschool children cannot remember complex instructions that include several things to remember. 'Go and fetch your shoes, your coat and your gloves' includes three things to remember. You will be lucky if he remembers one. So keep your requests simple and easy. If you want your child to help put away toys it is much easier for him to understand a specific request like 'let's put all of your cars in the box', rather than a general instruction to 'clear up' when he doesn't know where to put things.

- Clear positive consequences. 'Let's put your pyjamas on and then I'll read you a story' gives a very clear indication to the child about the sequence of events. The consequence needs to be something that your child wants to do, as it is being used as an incentive. If you listen carefully to yourself you may find that you actually say, 'If you don't put your pyjamas on, I won't read you a story', which is a threat rather than a positive consequence. The problem with this threat approach is that it includes two negative statements. It points out to the child what he should not be doing and then threatens the withdrawal of a reward that he has not yet had. It is hard to co-operate happily with negative motivation. Stating the positive provides a much more cooperative and warm interaction between you.

- Monitor cooperation. This means keeping an eye on whether he is doing what you have asked. We all too frequently make a request and then walk away because we have other things to do. We then find, 10 minutes later, that the child has not done what we wanted and feel cross that we have been ignored. When teaching young children to cooperate we have to stay throughout the whole process, prompt them and help them to do what we ask.

- Reinforce all attempts at cooperation. Young children are often not skilled enough to do what we want perfectly. They lose their concentration, they forget what they are supposed to be doing, and they are easily distracted from the task. They need to be praised and congratulated for any effort they make in order to keep them motivated and to keep them on the job.

- Physical and verbal prompts. In order to teach and help them cooperate they may need gently reminding or physically showing what to do. The task may need to be broken down into different components: 'Let's see if you can pick up the truck?', and then, once he has done it, 'OK, that's great, now put it in the box.' Taking turns, helping the child and encouraging the child to help you are all ways of speeding up the process.

- Humour, challenge and competition. Sometimes humour and saying the opposite gets the desired effect. 'I really don't want you to put on your pyjamas' can have a miraculous effect on a child rushing around with no clothes on at bedtime. 'I bet you can't get into the car before Lucy' will suddenly motivate a reticent 3-year-old who doesn't want to go shopping. Similarly, counting to three will help a child focus on speeding up or completing the job.

(Golding, 2000)

Should I punish him?

'I can't think of any more punishments that will work. What else can I do?' is a cry I hear from many parents who have got to the end of their tether and feel they are not in control of their children. They have started to move down into a negative spiral of threats, anger, and punishment. It is not what they ever meant to do, but desperation drives them into this blind alley. They want retribution. They are often aware that they are close to losing control of their emotions and their own behaviour if their child continues to be naughty, not do as he is told, or continue with temper outbursts. The volatility of the situation feels frightening for the adult; but I wonder how much worse it must feel for the child. They see their parents red-faced and screaming at them, their anger and irritation boiling over into statements that were never meant to be said:

- 'You are so wicked, I wish I'd never had you.'
- 'I'll leave you at your grandparents' house and they can look after you, because I can't stand you.'
- 'Why don't you ever leave me alone?'
- 'Get out of my sight I never want to see you again.'

Swear words come out, and you always vowed that you would never swear in front of the children. How do we get to such a pitch? How has this precious and loved baby become a little monster threatening your entire household and your sanity? We feel ashamed of what we say and do in the outburst. We apologise and try to make up. We end up feeling guilty and worried about the effect of our actions. But even more, does your child really understand why you felt so angry with him? Most preschoolers will not be able

to tell you what they did wrong. The final straw, which
made you erupt, was probably not that important. It was
the culmination of a series of events, which built up a
sense of frustration and helplessness, eventually resulting
in you losing your temper.

We use punishment and threat of punishment when
we have forgotten how to use positive approaches to child
management. Punishment means a penalty or a sanction
for bad behaviour. Technically it means doing something
unpleasant or aversive to your child as a consequence of
what they have done. The aim is for the punishment to act
as a way of stopping the child repeating the behaviour. For
punishment to work, any threat of punishment has to be
carried out. The problem is that parents use threats but
don't often carry them out. This leads to a confusing
situation and the child learns to ignore or challenge the
threat.

The other problem is that we have to be very clear
what the punishment is for. Quite often we are not
clear. The smack or threat of a smack happens when we
are feeling overwrought and upset rather than because our
child has done something really bad. The mother hauling
a crying child across the road shouting, 'I'll give you
something to cry for in a minute. Do you want a slap?',
has lost the whole point. It is a vent for emotion rather
than a teaching exercise. When you ask older children
about their experiences of being smacked by their
parents they can often remember the few incidents very
clearly but cannot remember why they were hit, only that
their parents were very angry. There is no real acceptance
of having been in the wrong. Men will often describe
beatings at school as the fair result of a prank, and will
say that they were stupid for having been caught. I
wonder whether the real effect is to make them better at
not being caught rather than deterring them from doing
the pranks.

Getting to the point of wanting to hit your toddler is a sign that things have gone way out of control and you need to sit down and think through what is happening. Much of your anger may be your problem, not your child's. So take stock, discuss it with your partner, and get help if you feel that you cannot control your feelings.

How do I manage his temper tantrums?

Tempers are very common in children aged between 18 months and 3 years. We talk about the terrible twos but this problem can start earlier and is linked to children becoming aware of themselves as separate beings with their own wants and desires. They become easily frustrated because they cannot control the world and find that a rage builds up in an uncontrollable fashion. They throw themselves on the floor, bang their heads, kick their legs, scream and shout and generally behave dreadfully. Your only hope at this stage is just to calmly ignore what is happening and, once your child has calmed down, sit with him, soothe him and think about the problem with him. It is pointless to shout at a child who is having a tantrum as he will not pay attention to you and will be unable to listen. The learning should take place once the tantrum has finished. You need to ensure that your child does not get his own way by losing his temper, and, if you have asked him to do something that he does not want to do, then you need to revisit that situation and start again so that he does learn to do what you say.

It is slightly more difficult out in public. Sometimes children become very adept at picking particularly embarrassing moments to have a tantrum if they are not given what they want. Of course, if you give way in order to keep him quiet, you are creating a huge problem for yourself and the tantrums will continue every time you go out and may even get worse. Your best plan is to try and ignore the behaviour as much as possible. Leave the shop so that you are not embarrassed by the noise in front of the other shoppers and walk down the street to a quiet corner until he calms down. Once he is quiet you should go back to the shop and finish what you were doing.

If tantrums are frequent, do try and check when they are happening to see if you can find a pattern. It may be related to loss of attention when the other children come home from school and your toddler no longer has you to himself. It may be related to worries at nursery. Some children who have a mild language delay or intermittent glue ear can show more tantrums as they are frustrated at not being able to communicate rapidly and easily. Some children find that screaming and tantrumming is a successful method of getting their own way.

Some children seem to have a very low threshold for boiling over in temper. Their volatile temperament may be a feature of someone in the family. They may need help to recognise how they feel. Labelling their feelings for them as they progress through the preschool years can be very helpful in teaching them to distinguish the differences in how they feel, so that not all emotional arousal comes out as anger. 'Sesame Street' the American children's programme used to be very good at teaching children labels for their emotions. Excitement, frustration, embarrassment, shyness, fear, worry are all related to feeling aroused emotionally, and children may have difficulties in saying how they are feeling.

Overhearing this little interaction one day made me realise how tangled up we become.

Child: *I want to go to the swings.*
Mum: *No, we can't, we need to go to the shops first.*

Child: (whining) *Ohhhh, Why?*

Mum: *We need to buy something to eat for tea.*

Child: *I don't want tea.*

Mum: *Don't be silly, of course you do.*

Child: (starts crying) *I don't want tea!*

Mum: (cross) *Oh, do be quiet! Or we won't go to the swings.*

Child: (crying loudly and banging legs in buggy) *Swings, swings, swings.*

The mother in this example perhaps should have thought more clearly whether a trip to the swings was possible before or after completing her shopping. It was in her mind, but she did not make it clear to her child. She said 'no' first and had already upset her child and then later used it as a threat for controlling bad behaviour, and both of them ended up losing their tempers.

Topical tips

- Setting limits for your child shows that you care.

- If you say 'no' then mean 'no'.

- Think before you speak.

- Carry through your requests.

- Stay calm and don't lose your temper.

- State clear incentives for cooperation.

- Prompt and praise all attempts at cooperation.

- Wanting to hit your child means that the situation is totally out of control. **Stop and Think**.

- You resort to punishment when you have forgotten how to use positive approaches to managing your child.

4

Family stress

No matter how keen you were to have a baby and no matter how happy your relationship is with your partner, you will experience considerable stress during the toddler years. The problems may come from a breakdown in your relationship with your partner, or from financial or housing difficulties, or may be related to learning how to cope with the demands of your toddler. If you fall apart then your toddler is left in a world of uncertainty with no one to care for him or her. As soon as you have children you shift into a different gear in terms of responsibility for others. You no longer just have to look after yourself; you have to look after your children as well. So coping with stress is a vitally important aspect of survival as a young parent.

Bringing a second baby home

Many parents feel unsure about how or when to broach the subject of having another baby with their 3-year-old.

They are worried about jealousy, about the 3-year-old feeling rejected and unloved. It is a transitional stage in the family, and all change produces a level of stress.

As soon as you are talking about the pregnancy within earshot of your child then you should tell him, so that you are not keeping a secret. Young children have great difficulty in understanding time and will have no concept of how long the pregnancy will be. They come to live with the prospect of a new baby coming, and they will see their preschool friends having new brothers and sisters.

Learning to cope with separation from Mummy will be an important issue on the agenda before the birth. So plan what is likely to happen around the time of the birth well in advance. Who will look after your toddler while you are in hospital? Will he stay at home or go to stay with someone while you are away? It can be very traumatic for some toddlers who have never experienced separation from their mother if it suddenly happens with no preparation at the birth of the next baby. Practise separation for gradually longer periods of time starting with about an hour and then increasing up to overnight with a relative or friend if necessary. If your partner is unable to take time off work then day care will still be an issue even if he is home at night.

The new baby arriving home is an exciting event. Your toddler will feel he is just as important as this new arrival and all of the visitors are equally his. He may become a bit overpowering and demanding with the excitement just when you are feeling a little vulnerable, and tired. It can help for the new baby to bring his older brother a special new toy when he comes home, and little girls often enjoy caring for a new doll in imitation of Mummy. Most visitors will be aware of the need to involve the toddler when they visit and may bring a present for him as well as the baby.

Reactions in toddlers can vary from a very caring and protective attitude to the new baby, to a rivalrous and aggressive response. Some children revert to becoming more baby-like. They revert to demanding a bottle again, perhaps want to breast-feed again, and may get up at night if they hear the baby crying and want to go into the parent's bed if that is where the baby is. Gentle and reassuring handling will get you through this; it won't last long if you help him to positively re-evaluate what he can do as an older child. Don't reject him or tell him to act more grown-up, but help him feel good about his abilities and recognise that his stage of development is just as exciting and interesting as the new baby growing and changing.

Involving your toddler in the care of the baby and talking about the baby as a person with feelings and pointing out the similarities between them will help your toddler feel more positive and warm. Take care not to let your toddler become too confident and walk around holding the baby without close supervision. Some parents, in an effort to be careful about their toddler's feelings, end up putting their baby at more risk than is desirable. Your toddler can hold the baby sitting on his lap under supervision.

Caring for more than one

As soon as you have two children your attention as a parent becomes divided. While you are attending to one, the other can get up to mischief. You can feel split in half and very irritable when you cannot maintain control. You expect the older one to show some sense or awareness of the stress you are under, but of course he doesn't. Who should wait? How do you balance the needs of your older child to have help with their spelling while the younger one needs a bath and a bedtime story? You can't be perfect all of the time. You will snap and shout and feel stressed; it's normal occasionally, but not every evening.

- Step one. Try and stay as calm as possible. Try not to let your agitation and personal pressure add to the already noisy situation. Count to 10, and use relaxation or yoga tips to calm yourself.
- Step two. Reduce your expectations and self-imposed standards of what you expect yourself to do. You cannot do more than three things at once, no matter how hard you try. But don't set unrealistic standards of house cleanliness, perfect meal on the table, immaculately clean baby and perfectly tutored son all at 6 p.m.
- Step three. Ignore what you can do nothing about. If you are busy changing the baby and your toddler has tipped out his entire toy box, don't shout or get stressed – just deal with it later when you can.
- Step four. Don't try to be supermum/dad. Be realistic about being a busy parent, but keep your children's needs in focus and watch for their reactions to their hectic lifestyle. You may feel like a taxi-driver rushing from one activity to the next as Janie has swimming lessons, Tom has football practice and Suzie has Tumble Tots. They can eat their sandwiches in the car for tea while you rush from one class to the next.
- Step five. Ask for help if you need it and can get it. Your partner can take over some of the child care tasks if you ask. Your relatives, if they live close by, can always be asked during a time of stress. If you can afford it, buy in some help with child care even

if its only for an hour or two in the evening when you are most stretched.

'My children fight all of the time'

Just because your children are siblings does not mean that they have to like each other; but they do need to learn how to live with each other and tolerate each other. The old maxim that 'you can't choose your relatives but you can choose your friends' is important to remember. Children's temperaments can be like chalk and cheese in the same family, and they may be at opposite poles. In addition there is built-in inequality due to age differences, ability differences and differences in looks. Jealousy, rivalry and competition are what you should expect, and if it doesn't occur then you are lucky. Some siblings are great friends, they protect and support each other, and they love being together and play well, while others are continually squabbling, fighting and competing.

If you are busy in the kitchen and you suddenly hear a scream and the sounds of a fight from upstairs, your immediate reaction is to go and sort it out. You storm in telling them to be quiet and stop fighting and you are met with a barrage of:

'Mum she took my car.'

'Mum he hit me.'

'No I didn't, you kicked me.'

'Yes you did, Mum he hurt me.'

'No I didn't, you tell lies.'

and so on.

What do you do? How do you know what has happened? You are called in as judge and jury to pass a punishment on something you have no idea about. You were not there, you don't know who is telling the truth, but you want it to stop and for them not to repeat it. In these situations we use:

- our knowledge of previous similar events,
- a judgement of probability,
- our own prejudices,
- our own attitudes to child care,
- guesswork,
- our feelings.

If you know that your 5-year-old boy tends to hit your 3-year-old girl when he gets frustrated, you could make a judgement that he has done it again and tell him off because it is likely that he did it. If you feel that boys should not hit girls no matter how old they are, then you will always tell off your son. If you know your daughter is in a bad mood today, you might guess that she is instigating the fight and tell her off. If you are tired and moody you might shout at both of them. The truth is unless you were there and witnessed the whole interaction from the beginning and possibly even several interactions earlier when the initial problem was set up, then you haven't a clue who to punish.

Tim, aged four, kept scratching his brother's face. He would reach out to grab him if they were sitting side by side in the buggy and taking them to the shops was becoming a problem. The boys would fight and scream, pulling each other's clothes and pulling off

> *their hats. It became evident that every time they did this their mother would try to stop them by giving them a toy to hold or some food to hold in order to distract them and occupy their hands. Her response continued to make the situation worse until she started to ignore them and then gradually they stopped fighting.*

Children have excellent memories about slights and unfairness to themselves. If they feel that their sibling has been unfair to them then they can store up their revenge to take it out at a suitable moment later in the day.

Most squabbles will be around sharing and taking turns. It is difficult for young children to cope with this and, when they are up against a sibling who also has problems with sharing, then it is likely to be a volatile combination. Many parents try to be scrupulously fair and buy presents for each of their children at the same time, or try to buy the same for each child so that there is no competition. This is difficult with age differences or gender differences as the same toy is not always suitable. Whatever you do your children will find differences and unfairness. Have you ever seen nursery and infant age children fighting over chairs in the classroom, which all look identical to the adult, but one has a mark on it or a bit of paint scratched off it? Nothing is ever totally equal.

Sharing you is also a main bone of contention. They will fight to sit next to you at the table, they will fight for your attention, and they will fight to sit on your lap. They will fight about tiny privileges that you consider insignificant, but to them it can be the end of the world.

- Who sits in the front seat of the car rather than the back?
- Who sits in which car seat?
- Who chooses the story at bedtime?
- Who has first choice of the yoghurts?

It doesn't stop. Even if you try to be fair and encourage them to take turns, I can bet you will have forgotten who had the first choice last time. They won't forget; but one of them is likely to tell lies if he thinks he can get away with it.

The most important rule for parents is not to take sides in your children's fights because you will always get it wrong and end up making the situation worse than it was to begin with. No matter how strongly you feel that your children should not hit each other, they will use this 'weak' point in you to get you involved and try to make an alliance with you. Children have their own ability to judge how far to go. If they overstep the mark in one fight and end up getting hurt, they rapidly learn not to go so far next time and find another strategy for equalising the fight. But if parents become involved then the parent is seen as the arbitrator and controller of the interaction. Children will accelerate their level of aggression and screaming to involve the parents and then expect them to sort it out. This can result in one learning to shout very loudly or to hit the other surreptitiously. Usually the weaker one learns to scream loudly, but part of the problem is that he can also be the instigator of the problem and the parent always ends up blaming the child who was more physically aggressive. If one child then feels upset because he considers his parent has been unfair, he builds up resentment and takes it out on his sibling at the next available opportunity.

The golden rule

Do not get involved in your children's fights.

What can you do? Here is a range of possible solutions that you can use depending on the situation.

- Shout at both of them for having interrupted you, but say nothing about the fight.
- Remove the toy that is the cause of the problem so that both are punished for having involved you.
- Listen to the problem but don't take sides.
- Encourage them to think of alternative solutions to the problems rather than fighting. This needs working at and a lot of practice but is the most effective way of reducing fights (see Chapter 2).
- Teach them to avoid difficulties, e.g. show the older one to keep his precious toys out of reach of the younger one. Provide a lock on the older child's bedroom door so that the younger one can't go in and disrupt it.
- Ignore the shouts and fights and just turn up the TV If you intend to ignore the noise, then don't go and see what is happening if the noise gets louder or you will teach them to make more noise in order to attract your attention.
- Use privileges as rewards for good behaviour rather than rights to fight over. Sitting next to Dad at the dinner table can be earned for having been good during the morning. Sitting in the front seat of the car is earned by each in turn only if both behave well on their way to the car, don't race and don't squabble. If there is any fighting they both automatically

sit in the back. The choice of story at bedtime is given to the one who gets ready for bed the fastest and cleans his teeth properly.

- Split up the fight and put the children in separate rooms to calm down and then, when they are both quiet, they can go back to play together.

- Reward sharing, turn-taking and playing cooperatively whenever you can by positively commenting on it and helping them recognise that you are pleased and proud of them. Tell your partner how pleased you are with each of them in front of them. Particularly praise an older sib for playing well with a younger sib while you are able to get on and do a job in the home.

- Distract very young children from squabbles by introducing another activity for them to do away from their sibling.

- Watch your own assumptions and prejudices. Don't assume that the older child, the younger child or the boy is always in the wrong.

- Make sure that if one child has a friend to play with that the other one also has a friend to play with.

- Help safeguard precious possessions and be very clear about what the other child is not allowed to touch.

- Safeguard the rights of both children, regardless of age.

- Don't expect family outings always to be happy and perfect. Your children will have different likes and needs, so do split them up at times and you take out one while your partner takes out or stays with the other. You will find that you get on much better with one child on his own as he has your undivided attention.

- Guard against squabbles and fights being the main way in which your children gain your attention.

Marital unhappiness

Your relationship with your partner will have a great
impact on your child's emotional development and
behaviour. The more your young child witnesses you
shouting and arguing with each other the higher the likelihood that your child will start to show aggressive and
difficult behaviour (Webster-Stratton & Hammond,
1999). Exposure to parents' verbal anger and violence is
particularly disturbing to children. Preschoolers show
more distressed emotional reactions than older children
and are also likely to blame themselves for the conflict
(Covell & Abramovitch, 1987; Cummings & Davies,
1994). The more exposure they have the less emotional
control they develop themselves. Your child is just as
sensitive to your distressed feelings and the tone of your
relationship with your partner as he is to the open hostility
you have to each other. Your child will copy the way you
behave to each other. He will learn to be angry and hostile
to others; he will learn how not to manage conflict effectively; he will learn how not to negotiate. Is that what you
want him to learn?

Preschool children mostly do not understand that
people behave they way they do because of what they
think inside (Jenkins & Buccioni, 2000). They can see
the behaviour of their parents, the anger and the distress,
but don't know why they are reacting that way. They
don't see their parents as a married couple with their
own relationship, but only as parents. This leads them
into thinking that all of the conflict must be about parenting and so tend to relate all that happens to themselves.
Young children think in very realistic and concrete terms,
observing what is happening around them and watching
behaviour rather than attributing intention. They know

when someone is angry but don't know that there is a reason.

They also think in absolute terms, that only one person can be right, and so are likely to take sides without realising the impact on the other parent. This does not mean that they prefer one parent over the other but that they have limited understanding of the complexity of relationships. They also think that once the anger and the argument has stopped, then the problem is over. They have little awareness that the problem has not been resolved by parents going quiet.

When parents have difficulty in controlling their emotions, working out problems together and communicating well, they generally find it harder to deal with the stresses that life throws at them. If they don't manage marital arguments well, then they will find coping with parenting problems difficult. It is easy to fall into using punishment, telling off, criticism, force and confrontation as the main style of child management when they feel like this. This trap can be a deep pit, which leads into more behaviour problems in the child as he feels rejected, unloved and criticised. He demands attention by being noisier, naughtier and disobedient in order to elicit some predictable behaviour from his parents. Even though this may be being shouted at, at least it is being noticed. It is easy to see how this downward spiral becomes difficult to stop. The child is blamed for the bad behaviour, but where is it really coming from?

Recent research in parenting is pointing the way to helping parents work out their marital relationship more effectively (Webster-Stratton & Hammond, 1999). They need marital support, they need help with managing their anger and feelings, and they need help in learning how to communicate effectively. This will help them learn how to manage conflict and stress and also to solve problems that occur on a daily basis. So as parents we have to think carefully how much our own difficulties in our adult relationships will spill over into affecting our children.

Think about how you solve your everyday problems with your partner and whether you collaborate well.

- Can you agree about what the problem is?
- Can you both provide a range of possible solutions or do you each stick to one and consider that is the only possibility?
- Are you able to assess which solution is the best rather than push to get your own way or always give way to your partner?
- Can you agree on which is the best solution?
- Can you plan and implement it together?

If you are good at collaborating then you are likely to be good problem-solvers. You accept joint ownership of problems, you accept responsibility, you reinforce each others attempts to problem-solve and you probably feel very positive towards each other and also feel supported by each other.

The way in which we cope generally with problems does fall into several categories:

1 Confident coping. You feel that you can manage most problems that are thrown at you reasonably well, that you can solve problems within the family and face up to the problem. You accept that stress occurs and try to define the problem in a more positive way so that it can be managed.

2 Ineffective coping. You blame others for the problem. You show anger and irritation or feel depressed and cry when facing a problem. Your

emotions get in the way of thinking about how to cope.

3   Passivity. You avoid thinking about the problem and hope it will go away. You feel helpless and that whatever you do will have no effect. You give up and do not do anything.

4   Seeking help or advice. This can be from relatives, friends or neighbours and those outside the family.

We all use a different combination of these coping styles depending on the situation and the type of problem we are facing. We need a range of different skills; but if you find you are mostly using passive or ineffective styles of coping then you need to think carefully, seek help and talk it over with your partner. Your coping style may be different to your partner's and you may need to work out how to help and complement each others' strengths and weaknesses.

The communication style in your family plays a vital role in how you relate to each other and also manage problems. Think about your main communication style and find out which column you fit into in the table at the top of the opposite page.

Positive communication styles are obviously more effective and make people around you feel happier and safer. They also make others like you more and feel that you are a nice person to know. Your child will feel more supported and his self-esteem will grow when he understands how you appreciate him.

If your relationship with your partner is rocky then stand back and take stock of the problems you are having. Seek help if you cannot work it out together. You have to give in order to receive and secure relationships seem to be

Positive communication	Negative communication
Say 'yes'	Say 'no'
Praise	Threaten
Appreciate	Force
Thank	Ignore
Humour	Deny responsibility
Smiling and laughter	Withdraw
Congratulate	Find fault
Compliment	Criticise
Cuddle/stroke/kiss	Blame
Help/support	Complain
Agree	Whine/moan/nag
Accept responsibility	Command
Welcome	Disagree
Good eye contact	Frown
Pay attention	Poor eye contact
Enjoyment	Rejection
Warmth	Avoidance
Enthusiasm	Flatness of emotion

slightly too easy to slip out of these days. It takes work and effort to keep a relationship steady with both of you seeing it as important to protect and maintain. If nothing else, learn to control your own anger. Don't let a sense of resentment build up, take responsibility for your feelings and sort out the problem.

Separation and divorce

Separation and divorce are a fact of life these days and many young children are caught up in their parents splitting up or divorcing. Sadly, divorce in early childhood is associated with long-term increases in anxious, hyperactive, disobedient and defiant behaviour later in childhood (Pagani *et al.*, 1997).

Young children often have no real understanding of what is happening but feel distressed by continual arguments and moods in the house. Your emotional state will have a considerable impact on your child. Your preoccupation with your worries, your depression or your anger will affect how you relate to and manage your child's behaviour. He will be aware that you are unhappy and may even try to get in the middle and solve the problems by diverting attention onto himself. I have seen many families where the child's misbehaviour is the main reason for the parents staying and working together as they try to sort out their child's problems. Of course there is no gain for the child to start to behave well, as the parents will no longer have a joint focus but will start to think about their own relationship problems again.

The child often becomes a pawn in the game of separation and divorce. Both parents want to have access and fight each other for time with the child. All the child ever wants is for the parents to live together again, and he may harbour this hope for many years, well after the parents have totally disregarded any possibility of that ever happening. They are then surprised when, even several years later, they start to make a new relationship with another partner that the child seems unduly distressed and misbehaves badly. It is the final abandonment of any hope that their parents will ever reunite and it is a very painful experience.

Young children have a simple understanding of what constitutes family membership and it is usually related to living in the same house together. If one parent leaves the home the young child may feel that the parent is no longer theirs and may become very anxious or worried about being left. Preschool children can show considerable behavioural regression with increased clinging, increased bedwetting and babyish behaviour. They desperately need reassurance and containment. They need to see where the parent who is leaving is going to live; they need to know that they are going to see them again and again. If they are not going to see that parent again, then that needs to be clear so that the process of bereavement and loss is properly worked on and understood. The remaining parent may feel angry and bitter, but the child feels bereft and sad. One of the most important issues to make absolutely clear to the child is that he is in no way to feel any sense of blame for the break-up of the relationship. Some children harbour the thought that their dad left home because they had been naughty. Parents must accept all of the blame for the break-up, and the child needs reassurance that both parents do love them and that they split up because they did not love each other any more.

The experience of separation and divorce can vary markedly from family to family. In some cases it is acrimonious and vitriolic with partners bearing resentment and anger towards each other. In other families it can be reasonably amicable with both parents accepting a sense of responsibility towards the children and trying to make the whole experience as manageable for them as possible. The pain that you feel from the break-up is yours to contain and should not be loaded onto your child; he has his own sense of upset. The emotions that you feel towards your previous partner are yours to contain; your child feels differently. Some children are forcibly drawn into the parental conflict with unpleasant comments being made to the child about the other parent in an effort to point out to the child the defects and blame for the unhappiness (Dowling & Gorell-Barnes, 1999).

You may be keen to start another relationship, and may even have a new friend who you hope will become more permanent. It can be a problem to decide when to introduce this new person to your children. You may want to protect them from the number of short-term relationships that you may have and only want them to become involved with the long-term possibilities. The difficulty you have to face is that you will know your new partner far better than they will by the time you finally introduce them. It will be very tempting to speed up their acceptance of the new member of the family, but your children need time and patience. They are likely to be resistant, unsure, suspicious and jealous. They may reject the new partner or may fight him in order to protect you.

Sasha was having great problems with Mark, her 3-year-old, who was waking at night and ending up in her bed every night. Her relationship had ended the previous year with Mark's father and she was keen to make a go of a new relationship that was developing. Her new boyfriend stayed on some nights and Mark's sleep problem was causing her a lot of worry, as she did not want him to know that the boyfriend was staying.

Parenting apart

There can be ongoing struggles and resentment about different child-management styles, expectations and rules after you break up. You can only try to parent the best way you know how; you cannot control the behaviour of your ex-partner. Your child will grow to realise that you have different views and will learn to behave differently according to the expectation of each parent. You may feel very angry and resentful that your ex-partner lets your child stay up later than you think he should, gives your child the wrong food, is teaching him bad manners or keeps buying lots of presents. You can do nothing about this and so worrying and getting upset will only hurt you. We all learn to behave according to the circumstances and expectations of the environment in which we live; children are no different. Worry about what you can control and not what you can't control (Hetherington & Stanley-Hagan, 1999).

In unhappy separations parents often worry about what one partner is saying about the other partner to the child. They worry that they are being blamed, slandered or criticised inappropriately. All you can do is stick to your own values and not fall into the trap of criticising your ex when talking to your child. If you keep your negative thoughts to yourself you will find that, as your child grows older, he will respect you for not having loaded him with your anger and resentment. He will form his own opinion of his parents' good and bad qualities, which is bound to be different to your evaluation of your ex, with whom he will have a different relationship.

You can't really protect your child from disappointment if your ex is inconsistent in seeing him, in phoning or in sending cards and presents at birthdays. You can only do what you can do, which is to provide a caring and loving home with consistency and support. You may feel torn up inside when you see him upset and want desperately to prevent him from feeling like this; but being negative about your ex at this time will only make your child feel defensive of your ex. You need to keep your child's feelings in mind and help reassure him that he is loved by both of you, but that each of you shows it differently and just that your ex can be very forgetful at times. If you show distress or anger then your child is having to cope with your feelings as well as his own.

Parenting apart can work successfully if separated parents develop a mode of communication that is clear, non-blaming and focused on the child's needs rather than their own. Scoring points off each other only hurts your child, so think how best your child can be supported by you both. Work out your agreed access arrangements. Be prepared for some flexibility as life changes for both of you and you move into different relationships with new partners. Be clear about holidays, what to do on parent's evenings at nursery or school, who goes to school plays and concerts. Your child belongs to both of you but don't tear him in two.

Topical tips

- Siblings do not have to like each other.

- Don't take sides in your children's fights.

- Nothing is ever totally equal or fair.

- Encourage your children to think of different solutions to the problem rather than fighting.

- Don't expect family outings always to be happy and perfect.

- Your child will copy how you behave to each other.

- Young children often feel responsible for their parents' separation.

- Your child feels differently towards your ex than you do.

- You cannot control how your ex manages your child.

- Your child belongs to both of you; don't tear him in two.

- Think about what you can control and not what you can't control.

5

Is my child overactive?

There is a lot of anxiety among many parents that their toddlers may have ADHD. This term, 'attention deficit hyperactivity disorder', has become a common diagnosis among older, school-age children and is replacing the term 'hyperactive' as it is more precise in its description. ADHD is a psychiatric diagnosis of a particular behavioural disorder in children, and any diagnostic category has to exclude and include cases. The problem for parents is the point of exclusion. You may have a child who has problems with attention and is very overactive, but he may not meet the precise requirements for the diagnosis. This does not take away the fact that you are dealing with a child who is hard to handle and wears you out. Also this diagnostic category does not apply to preschool children. Young children show such a wide range of levels of activity and concentration that it has been difficult clearly to diagnose this disorder in this age group. The other feature of a psychiatric label such as ADHD is that it links to a particular treatment that has been found to be valuable. Medication has been found to be particularly

beneficial to older children with ADHD but it is not pre-
scribed generally under the age of 6 years (Campbell,
1990).

So we are left with a situation where we need to look
closely at young children's behaviour in a variety of
contexts and in relation to their developmental stage.
We are not pursuing a diagnostic category with this age
group of preschoolers. But it is obvious that ADHD does
not suddenly erupt at 6 years of age: the signs are going to
be there earlier in childhood (Campbell & Ewing, 1990).

Concentration and attention

Attention and concentration are key skills that allow a
child to learn. It is very difficult to learn anything new if
you lose your concentration every few seconds or if you
cannot attend long enough to reach the end of the task.
But, as you already realise, children's attention and concentration is limited in the preschool years, and it is
through a mixture of teaching and maturation that children are able to extend these powers as they grow older.
Your 1-year-old will flit through the toy basket, tipping it
out, picking up a few toys for a few minutes, mouthing
them and then leaving them for something else. But your
3-year-old will be able to sit and play with a toy for up to
half an hour if he is really interested and can make up a
game to go with it.

The problem is there are no clear guidelines for how
long children should be able to concentrate at each age.
Psychological assessments of children's levels of functioning are much more related to what they can do rather than
how they do it. The problem is that concentration is often
related to interest and motivation. Your 2-year-old may

be able to sit still and listen to a story if it is read with funny voices, in a book with lots of pictures to keep him involved and sitting on your lap feeling tired at the end of the day. But if he is busy and wants to do his own play and you try and make him sit still to listen to a boring story with no pictures, I wonder how long he would last. There are so many different issues that affect young children's concentration that it is very difficult to draw any strong guidelines (Egeland *et al.*, 1990).

What affects concentration?

1 Age
Concentration improves with age.

2 Maturation level
Concentration improves with higher maturation.

3 Gender
Boys often have poorer concentration than girls in the early years.

4 Interest
Low level of interest results in low concentration.

5 Length of activity
Several short tasks are easier to concentrate on than one long one.

6 Difficulty of the activity
It is harder to concentrate on a difficult task than a simpler one.

7 Type of activity
Passive attention is more difficult than active

attention when the child is joining in and doing something.

8 Motivation
   When your child does not want to cooperate he will have poor concentration.

9 Distraction
   Young children are easily distracted, so high levels of potential distraction will reduce concentration levels.

10 Physical state
    Irritation, pain, hunger, needing to go to the toilet, tiredness, having an itch will all reduce concentration.

11 Emotional state
    Anxiety, excitement, boredom and fear all reduce concentration levels.

If you feel that your child is showing poor concentration, then it is important to try and assess it in different situations and while doing preferred activities. I have seen parents who are concerned about their 4-year-old's concentration as he won't complete a puzzle, but then find that he can sit and watch his favourite video for half an hour with no problem. A child can find it difficult to complete a task on his own, but if a parent is paying attention, prompting and helping, he is able to maintain his concentration for much longer periods. But don't forget that if you take over and do it all for him then he will lose his concentration even more rapidly.

Distraction is very disruptive to attention and concentration, so if you want your child to concentrate, it is important to try and reduce the level of distraction as

much as possible. One thing that we all do as parents is to
provide too many toys all at the same time. No wonder
they tip out all of their boxes and flit from one toy to the
next without seeming to enjoy playing with them. Toys
are easily broken if there are too many on the floor and
they are trodden on.

*Simi, aged four, was described as a tornado by his
mother. He would empty all of his toy boxes onto the
floor and then just walk all over them, or ride his
bike over them and break them, which made her
angry. She spent her time clearing up after him
and was exhausted and frustrated. He was a very
lively boy who flitted between activities. He would
demand to do painting and by the time she had
cleared the kitchen table ready to paint he would
have lost interest and gone off to do something
else.*

*We discussed how she could put most of his toys
away in the cupboard and have out only a limited
number at any one time, to try and stop him flitting.
His mother agreed to sit down with him and show
him how to use the toys and start him off on con-
struction activities, helping him when he couldn't do
it and encouraging him to stay with one activity as
long as possible before he went onto the next. If he
needed to run off for a short break, that was fine; but
she could encourage him to come back to the joint
activity they were doing if she waited and was
patient. They also learned to put one set of toys
away before another set was brought out. So
tidying up became a joint effort and a game, with*

*the prospect of new toys to play with once he had
cooperated.*

*He was stopped from riding his bike indoors, but
she made time each day to take him out so that he
could ride it in the garden. She learned to structure
their time together so that they had quiet activity
times and then large physical activity times outside
at the park or in the garden.*

*She found that his behaviour improved and he was
able to achieve more enjoyment when she helped him
as he didn't become so frustrated.*

You can help develop your child's ability to concentrate and persevere with activities by being very clear
yourself about what you want him to be able to do. If
his flitting prevents him from completing any activities,
then think about the list above and plan some simple
activities that you know he enjoys. Time how long he
can stay on task and then just put it on one side if he
runs off. After he has played with some other toys, encourage him to come back and join in the task again.
Gradually he will realise that he can eventually finish a
task like a puzzle and gain some sense of achievement and
satisfaction. If you know how long he can last, you can try
to increase his ability to stay doing the task for a minute or
two longer. Gradually you can build up the length of his
concentration time.

One of the main reasons that parents worry about their
child's attention span is that, when he is naughty, he
doesn't appear to listen to what is being said. You ask
him to go and get his coat but he runs off and does something else instead; he won't sit at the table for meals; he
runs off at bedtime and won't get changed for bed. Some-

times it is very difficult to know whether your child is just being disobedient or whether he has not heard the instruction. It is very important to ensure that your child has heard and understood what you have asked.

Young children have a limited memory for a sequence of instructions. A 2-year-old can follow a simple single command like 'put the cup on the table', while a 4-year-old can follow an instruction to do three things in order in one command like 'put this cup on the table, put the spoon in the drawer and bring me a plate' – that is if they are feeling cooperative.

As parents we often embed one instruction inside another, which can confuse young children. We have to learn to be clear and concise in our demands, using language that our children can understand and not adding in extra information that just makes them forget what we have asked. To ensure that you gain his attention and compliance, ensure that he is looking at you when you ask him to do something, remove him from distractions, encourage him to repeat back what you have said and watch whether he does as you ask.

Frustration and aggression

Some children are thought to be overactive because they have a limited ability to control their emotional outbursts. They get angry very rapidly, lose their tempers and can be physically aggressive – kicking, hitting, pulling hair or clothes, biting and throwing toys. They draw attention to themselves in playgroup because of this loud and difficult behaviour, and at home they can be difficult to manage as their parents can feel frightened by the intensity of their reaction. Asking them to do something, or to stop doing something, can provoke an outburst, and so it is tempting to try and keep the peace by not frustrating them in any way. Gradually they gain more and more control by their violent and aggressive behaviour. Parents and other children learn to back off and let them have their own way, and they gradually become more uncontrollable. This is not overactive or hyperactive behaviour, is it just naughty behaviour; and if this is happening then you need to learn how to get back in charge. Using the ideas we discussed in Chapter 3 will help. But there are a few children who behave in this way because they are unhappy and distressed within themselves.

Being active

A preschooler who is starting to show the signs of ADHD will be restless, irritable, very active, unable to complete tasks, flitting from one activity to the next and unable to join in with other children in any group game. They will barge into other children without realising and will get a reputation for being rough. They will be easily frustrated, and this can often turn to anger and leads them to tearing up work or throwing or destroying toys. The very high activity level in all situations is the most important distinguishing factor.

But don't forget that young boys are generally much more physically active and rumbustious than little girls of the same age. So do check out the activity level of other boys of the same age before you start making assumptions. Just because your 4-year-old boy can climb your garden fence in two minutes does not mean that he is overactive. Boys love large activity toys like bikes and cars; they love high-energy games like ball games; they will run and chase each other. But they will get tired and will relax and have a quiet time as well. But children who have ADHD seem to get more over-excited by physical activity and tend to get more active and irritable rather than tired and quiet.

Impulsivity is another feature of children with ADHD. But, as you already realise, young children are generally quite impulsive. They don't think through consequences and often don't recognise danger. Your job as a parent of a preschooler is to look out for danger for him, to point it out and help him learn how to behave. You are there to prevent him from running out onto roads, climbing on unsafe structures or doing any of the million other dangerous activities that preschoolers appear to enjoy. Gradually your child will learn to recognise danger, but children with ADHD don't seem to learn in the same way. Their impulsivity continues and so they seem more immature in their ability to recognise danger as they grow older. It is as if they have no self-control and are ruled by the impulse of the moment. Parents often question why it seems that their child does not learn by his experiences as others do. The spur of the moment seems to take over without any regard as to what might happen.

How to cope

It is very easy to become stricter, to tell off your child more and to feel exasperated and angry with him when he is continually demanding, overactive, disobedient and impulsive (Woodward *et al.*, 1998). He can wear you out and yet still have energy to keep going for several more hours. It is easy to start to see all of the problems rather than the positive times. You wonder why he never does what you say; everything seems to be a battle and you feel incompetent as a parent. This can turn to anger and resentment towards your child. You go to bed at night crying and vowing to try better the next day, but within half an hour of him waking up in the morning you feel dreadful again.

To cope with these problems you need to:

- remain focused on your child's needs,
- be able to express warmth and affection towards your child,
- be able to reason and communicate openly,
- set and enforce rules and boundaries,
- avoid being over harsh or restrictive or using punishment excessively.

(Woodward *et al*., 1998)

Parents of hyperactive children tend to feel more negative about them and see the problem as being the child's. But this negative attitude tends to lead to more aggressive and reactive discipline styles, which are generally less effective methods of coping in the long term. If you look back in Chapters 2 and 3, those principles still hold and you need to apply them consistently. You need to:

- anticipate problems before they arrive,
- be proactive to reduce the likelihood of problems,
- be positive and use incentives to encourage good behaviour,
- ignore the difficult behaviour if possible and comment on the good bits that you see,
- reduce the level of demands or commands that you say to your child,
- carry through your requests and ensure that your child complies,
- keep a lid on your temper and not shout,

- give yourself a break and share the child care duties if possible,
- reduce your expectations of yourself and your child; set small goals so that you can both succeed,
- do not leave your child unattended, he needs monitoring at all times,
- try to remain calm and see the humorous side of life.

Sometimes this is easier said than done. Overactive pre-schoolers can and will wear you out, and test your patience to the limit (Douglas, 1991).

Jimmy, aged four, caused havoc at bedtime as his parents had developed a routine of bathing both of their children together before bed. He would become so over-excited that he would splash the bathwater out of the bath and soak his parents and the carpet. He thought this was great fun and never seemed to understand the consequences that his parents would become angry. The impulsive action was too great for him to control. His parents devised a new routine of bathing his sister first and then only having 2 inches of water in the bath and keeping him much calmer without his sister present.

One important difference with children who are hyperactive is that they do need very immediate and regular feedback about their behaviour. The rewards and praise need to be frequent and rapid. They are unable to hold on to the thought that they have been good for any length of time and regular rewards do not lose their incentive value as they do with other children. So you will need to learn how to keep on being positive all of the time.

Structure and planning is also very helpful in managing life at home with hyperactive preschoolers. They do need a tremendous amount of attention and guidance. Routine and structure will help you and them anticipate what is going to happen. Avoid problems whenever you can see a repetitive pattern developing. When your other children come home from school, you may find your toddler going wild. The excitement, the distraction, the stimulation will all encourage more overactive behaviour. Trying to control him at this time is likely to be a lost cause, so accept it and try to protect the other children from the demands of your lively one. Split parenting at weekends can be helpful, and allow your other children an opportunity for uninterrupted time with you. Don't forget that you also need a rest, so encourage your partner to take over for a few hours.

Hyperactive preschoolers are very exhausting and can cause considerable strain in families. Try to keep calm, let some things go and provide as much attention and structure as you can. Look for small successes and notice when he does as he is told. He needs lots of praise and positive feedback when he is doing well. He is not doing this deliberately to you; he finds it nearly impossible to control his impulsivity, so he needs you to keep him safe and manage him calmly when things gets out of control. He will be sorry and show remorse, but will do it again next time. He needs to learn, so you need to keep on and on teaching him how to behave.

Topical tips

- ADHD is not diagnosed in preschool children.

- Attention and concentration improve with maturation in most children.

- Reduce the level of distraction to enable better concentration.

- Check that your child has paid attention to, heard and understood what you say.

- Structure and routine at home will help.

- Impulsivity makes them unaware of danger.

- Hyperactive children need more frequent rewards and positive feedback.

- Your child is not behaving like this deliberately.

6

Eating and your child

Battles over food are part of life with young children. About a quarter of mothers think that their preschooler has a problem with eating. They may be being fussy about what their child eats or that he does not eat enough, but it still causes worry. Mothers, in particular, feel very emotionally involved with how and what their child eats. This links back to the early months of breast- and bottle-feeding where she mostly had primary responsibility for feeding the baby. Checking on the quantity that the baby feeds and relating it to how the baby is growing and thriving is very much the mother's role, and it is all too easy for her to feel blamed if her baby is not growing sufficiently well.

Weaning

Taking your baby through weaning is another hurdle that is overcome in the first year. Some babies accept purées and the spoon with alacrity while others resist, spit, fight and cause concern and distress. Generally, babies start to be weaned some time between 4 and 6 months of age. There is no rush to do this. It can be done gradually as your baby becomes used to the new idea and the new sensations. Offering a tiny taste of purée on your finger before a feed is often the starting point. Even mixing some breast milk with baby rice is an early first step that allows your baby to manage a new texture with a familiar taste. Gradually increasing the amount offered and moving to a spoon when your baby is happy makes the transition relaxed. Babies have a very strong tongue thrust when they are primarily teat feeding, as it is those tongue reflexes that help to strip the teat of milk. So don't be worried if everything you seem to get into your baby's mouth keeps coming out again with the tongue thrust. This does not mean your baby doesn't like the food; it is just that he has not yet learned how to keep the food in his mouth.

Giving up breast-feeding

If you have to go back to work within your baby's first six months, you will need to teach him to transfer onto a bottle; if it is after this time, then you can probably transfer him straight onto a teacher beaker and miss out the bottle. Change can be resisted, even at this young age; but if you persevere he will cope. The biggest problem is likely to be your sense of guilt or upset at having to create a change before you feel that he is ready to do it. You also may feel very sad that the special phase is coming to an end.

Some mothers do not have to make this decision and

carry on breast-feeding into the second and third years of
life. They are prepared to wait until their child decides
that he no longer wants to breast-feed. Whichever route
you choose, you need to feel comfortable. I have seen
mothers who are desperate to stop breast-feeding their
toddlers, but find that the child's demands are too
strong. Other mothers have been happy to continue
breast-feeding but their child is not thriving sufficiently
without a solid diet and the continual snacking at the
breast on demand is reducing the toddler's appetite for
any other food. It is important to establish a balance, so
that both you and your child's needs are met. You can take
control of this situation as you are in charge of access to
the breast and to food. Your child needs a balanced diet
that meets his nutritional needs. As a baby and toddler he
will not be able to choose this: you have to choose it for
him.

Solid foods

Moving on to trying different textures of food towards the
end of the first year is another transition that can cause
problems. Some babies resist the earlier move onto lumpy
purée. They spit out lumps, gag and refuse to eat anything
but the smooth purée they have become used to. They
need to learn how to cope with soft lumps of food safely
and without gagging. Reducing the liquid content of the
purée makes it more sticky. Mashing soft root vegetables
will make the purée more textured and your baby won't
find a pea or a piece of carrot in the midst of the purée,
which is often a problem with stage 2 jar foods. The more
gradual change in texture will often work and help your
child adjust to the new demands of the food in his mouth.

Finger foods are usually introduced by the end of the first year by offering small pieces of biscuit, rusk, or cooked soft vegetable that your child can pick up and eat with his hands. Most of this will disappear over the edge of the tray onto the floor in a game designed to engage you in picking it up. If you whisk it off to the bin because it's dirty, you'll be met with howls of dismay – until he finds the next bit to hurl to the ground. This is an opportunity for your toddler to really explore and feel the texture. He needs to squash the food, make a mess and thoroughly enjoy himself and then lick his fingers. He will start to put food in his own mouth through this process. The first solid foods should be ones that dissolve down to a paste in saliva. Rusks and rich tea biscuits are ideal as the baby has the idea of sucking on something solid but there are no pieces that can cause him to gag. As he becomes more adventurous, he may bite off pieces; but they will rapidly dissolve in his mouth. If you eat your meal with him you will be able to offer tastes from your plate and so broaden his experience of tastes and textures without cooking specially for him.

Self-feeding

You can really interrupt and interfere with the development of self-feeding if you want to. If you are anxious about avoiding mess and keep wiping your toddler's hands and face while he is eating, he will learn gradually that it is not a good idea to have messy hands and become anxious himself about touching food. He may then be reluctant to pick up food in his hands but may not have the skills to manage cutlery well enough. He may then revert back to being spoon-fed by you, and a more dependent and infantile pattern continues. So do try and wait until the end of the meal before you wipe your child's face and hands. It should be a signal that the meal is over, not a concern about mess.

The other way of interrupting this transition to self-feeding is fighting over the spoon. Parents who are worried about the quantity that their child is eating like to stay in charge of the spoon, because then they know how much their child has actually eaten rather than tipped into his bib or smeared on the tray. But towards the end of the first year your toddler will want to take charge himself. There is often an interesting period of several spoons at each mealtime: you have one or two, and he has one or two; some get thrown on the floor; but usually most of the food ends up in his mouth, either on your spoon or his. Loading his spoon for him can help, and gently guiding his hand, if he will let you, to make sure it gets into his mouth with food still on, it is an art. If you start to fight over the control of the spoon, you may find that you have a child who refuses to cooperate and won't eat because he is cross and frustrated.

> *Ben, aged 18 months, was refusing to eat the food his mother offered at meals. When the meal was observed, his mother put toys on his high-chair tray to distract him while she stood to one side with his bowl of food and tried to spoon-feed him. When he saw the food coming towards him he tried to grab the spoon, but his mother slapped his hand away and told him that he could not have it. He then became cross and turned his head away from the spoon. His mother pointed out how he was refusing to eat and became upset herself.*

My child is a fussy eater

Toddlers go on and off food with astonishing speed. What
they eat one day they may refuse the next. Food fads are
common and most parents manage this by ignoring it. As
long as he eats something at the meal it does not really
matter if he has not had everything that you have prepared
for him. Just reintroduce the rejected food a few days later
to see if the fad has gone. Sometimes watching you eat
with relish the food that he has rejected may make him
keen to have it back again.

The major problem is that you have thought of,
shopped for and cooked a meal, some of which is being
rejected. This hurts. It's a waste of time and effort and he
had better eat it or else. Your need to see your child eat
happily and finish his plate is your main motivating force,
and when he doesn't it is easy to fall into cajoling him,
nagging him, commanding him to eat, or threatening punishment if he doesn't eat. You imagine someone doing that
to you. Would it make you eat and enjoy your meal? Can
you remember sitting at the table as a child with something in your mouth that you couldn't make yourself
swallow because you didn't like it? Were you shouted
at? Were you forced to eat food you didn't like because
it would be wasted? Were all the starving children in
Africa mentioned to make you feel guilty? How did you
feel?

If you can break away from the feeling that your child
is rejecting you when he is rejecting your meal, then you
have managed step one. This is not a personal issue, and it
shouldn't be an emotional one. If your child is an appropriate weight and healthy, then it doesn't matter if he
misses the odd meal or refuses to eat certain things on
his plate. He will eat at the next one when he is hungry,

as long as you don't fill him up on sweets, drinks and crisps to compensate. If he realises that he can get these if he doesn't eat at meals, then what is he likely to do?

> *Peter, aged four, was normal weight and height for his age. His mother was very worried that he never ate his meals and would run away from the table at mealtimes. She reported that he never ate anything, but it was clear from the fact that he was thriving that he was eating. She kept a daily diary for three days of everything that went in his mouth, including all snacks, sweets and drinks both during the day and at night. The diary revealed that he was having a range of crisps, biscuits, cheese dippers, yoghurts and 3 pints of milk over 24 hours, 2 pints of which he had during the night in a bottle. His weight was being maintained by the snacks and milk, so his mother had to reconsider totally how she was offering him food in order to focus his hunger into mealtimes.*

Some parents get so caught by their own desire to see their child eat that they start to offer their child something else to eat and get trapped into cooking another meal and sometimes yet another meal if the second one is rejected. In some families a pattern evolves where the members of the family have learned to be so faddy that they all eat different foods and three or four different meals are cooked each evening to cater to everyone's individual preferences. The mother has tried to meet everyone's needs but not asserted her own: that it is a ridiculous amount of unnecessary work to do all of that cooking. If you suspect that you have these tendencies, then stop and think. If you pander to the whim of your child about what he will and will not eat, then you are creating a difficult situation for yourself, which is likely to continue for some time. You are passing over control to your child and allowing him to choose his meals (Budd *et al.*, 1998).

We are talking about toddlers, and I wonder how many times you have asked your 3-year-old what he wants to eat. Can he really give you a menu plan? Does he really know the range of marvellous culinary possibilities that exist? Of course not. So why ask? He will be very limited in what he knows and so he will stick to the same foods, chicken nuggets and chips, every day.

If your child has become seriously faddy and has maintained a very limited diet for more than six months without change then it is important for you to take this seriously. Some preschoolers can be very selective about what they eat, to the extent that it starts to impinge on their social life. They refuse to go to tea with friends and refuse to go to parties. They make it impossible for the family to eat out at a restaurant and, eventually, they have a problem when they start school and cannot eat school dinners. This problem can become a very long-standing one.

In addition to being selective about the food they are prepared to eat, children can also become selective about the brands of food or the packaging. It is very easy to lapse into selecting only the brands that your child will eat. But if you do this you are pandering to his control over your shopping and are not helping him to experience a wider range of tastes. Gradually he will become so rigid in what he will eat that he will refuse to eat any other version than his preferred brand. This limitation and inflexibility can start to interfere seriously with your freedom in the super-market. So be careful not to be in too much of a set routine in what you buy. Make sure that you try new brands, change brands, and encourage flexibility and exploration of tastes.

John, aged three, would only eat Walkers salt and vinegar crisps and no other brand or flavour. But, if the crisps were tipped out of the packet onto the plate in front of him he would not eat them. He would only eat them if he was taking them directly out of the packet.

Tim, aged 5 years, would only eat Mars bars if they were in their wrapper. They were his favourite food and he ate six a day. But if his mother put one on the plate not in its wrapper he refused to eat it.

Julie, aged 2 years, stopped eating yoghurts when the packaging changed. She could not be convinced that the contents had not changed.

If your child is starting to show problems of being selective, then be aware of the danger of being totally controlled by him. Your job is to keep the range of food options open. Ensure that he learns to have tiny tastes of foods that are not in his limited range. A tiny lick or a half-centimetre square of the new food is all he needs to have. But he may be very resistant and try to avoid cooperating by losing his temper, running off, crying or just being obstinate. He needs to learn to do as you ask. So we come back to the process of teaching your child to listen to what you say and obeying you.

Children are experts at developing strategies of behaviour that enable them to get their own way. They know which buttons to press that will make you give in. So watch the avoidance tactics that your child uses and think about how that makes you feel. If you can stand back from the situation and be more objective, you will be able to control your own feelings and then decide, in a more balanced way, which is the right strategy to take. If he cries and becomes upset just wait until he has calmed down; but don't start making a fuss of him or trying to pacify him. If he suspects that crying will weaken your resolve to get him to taste a new food he will keep on doing it and even cry louder. It is easy then to think that he might have a problem and is phobic or fearful of food. Your calm resolve will gradually win and your child will realise that his strategy does not work. He will realise that he needs to do as you say in order to have his preferred food, and will accept that having a small taste of a new food is not as dreadful as he had thought. But if you fluctuate in your decisions and give in he will win and remain a selective eater.

Try not to head into an all-out battle about this, and definitely keep calm and cool. The foods that you initially offer should be new brands of the same foods that he eats easily, e.g. Tesco's fish fingers rather than Sainsbury's; new flavours of foods that he enjoys, e.g. banana yoghurt as well as his preferred strawberry yoghurt; and foods that are very similar to the ones that he eats now, e.g. another type of biscuit, bread or cracker. Make your first steps easy and make sure that you succeed. If you don't set your sights too high you will win, and he will win by trying a new food and getting the food that he wants. It is very hard to jump straight from only eating chips to trying roast chicken or satsumas. But it is easier to move from eating white bread to brown bread or rolls. If you think of the range of foods as a ladder, you need to start at the bottom rung and work up, gradually increasing the range of foods that he eats and the amount that he eats of them. This takes time so you need to be prepared for a long haul. A very selective child can take several months to build up the confidence and ability to eat six or seven new foods without resistance.

All of this requires you to put in a lot of effort to be consistent, firm and calm. The continual drain on your energy and emotions each mealtime can be a considerable strain; but it does pay off if you keep at it. The worst scenario is if you make a request that your child refuses and then, after you both get upset, you let him get away with not trying the new food. All he has learned to do is to oppose you, and so next time you try it will be even harder. Also you have both become upset at the table and you can start to dread the strain of meals. You have probably heard many people say: do not make an issue out of food. That is true in terms of keeping calm and not losing your temper. But if your child is a selective eater, you do need to aware that you may be limiting your child's ability to try new foods by never encouraging him or expecting him to eat anything different from his preferred range.

My child eats so little

Most mothers tend to worry if their child does not eat as much as they think he should. Sometimes the problem is that your expectation of the quantity that your child should eat is greater than the amount he can manage. Many toddlers will miss occasional meals or show less interest, depending on how they feel. As long as your child is growing along the appropriate height and weight centiles for his age, he will be fine. If you look in your child's red Health Book, which you had from your GP, you will see graphs for height and weight. Your health visitor will have recorded on these your child's height and weight at the various visits you have had to the community health clinic. Weights that stay within the normal range, i.e. down to the 10th centile line, are generally nothing to worry about – as long as your child's weight has not taken a sudden dive down from above the 50th centile. Illness will affect children's appetite as much as it affects yours, so some weight loss is explainable and will be recovered when your child feels better. Your child's weight is also related to his birth weight, the parents' heights and weights and to any medical condition that he has.

If you think that your child has a small appetite, then it is probably worth keeping a food and drink diary for a week and record everything that he eats and drinks in every 24 hours. You may find that, over the course of a day, he is in fact taking in far more than you thought. He may be snacking in small amounts throughout the day and taking the edge off his appetite. He may be drinking sugary or milky drinks regularly throughout the day, which also can diminish his appetite. It is very easy to leave a beaker of juice out all day, that your toddler can help himself to, without realising that it might affect how much he eats. If you want to leave out a drink then leave out water and he will drink this if he is thirsty, but it will not affect his appetite. Some children fill up on drinks at the beginning or during a meal, so it also can be helpful to offer a drink after the meal is finished rather than during the meal.

Another way of increasing appetite is to offer small portions of different foods in succession during the meal. You know that if you are faced with a huge plate of spaghetti that it can feel a bit boring by the end; but if you have different flavours and textures of food on your plate, then it is easier to eat a lot more. Interest, anticipation and difference can all improve appetite. So put a small quantity on his plate to begin with, much less than you think he should eat. After he has finished you can be really pleased and praise him for finishing and then produce a small amount of pudding and then a few crisps and then a few chocolate buttons and so on until he really is full. The change and the introduction of something new can really interest a toddler and maintain him eating for longer. Also, the fact that you are praising him for finishing his plate, rather than nagging, forcing or shouting, helps him to feel happier and more relaxed about meals.

My child refuses to eat

Refusing to eat is a general statement that can include a variety of different problems. It can mean:

- refusing food but drinking a lot of milk or juice,
- refusing to eat what you provide on the table but eating at other times,
- refusing to accept you putting the spoon in his mouth because he wants to do it himself,
- refusing certain textures of foods, e.g. solid or finger foods as opposed to purée,
- loss of appetite due to current illness,
- long-term and chronic low appetite leading to serious weight problems.

It is important to try and decide what the problem is. Young children do not refuse food entirely unless there is a serious medical problem, and then they lose weight dramatically. Check your child's weight at your health clinic and look at the weight graphs and see whether they are progressively dropping down the centile lines. If they are, then you need to see your GP.

If your child's weight is fine, then consider carefully his pattern of eating and drinking throughout the day, using a diary. Ways of tackling the other reasons for food refusal in normal-weight children can include:

- Restrict milk and juice and offer water during the day/ restrict bottles at night.
- Don't allow snacks in the house and stop your child helping himself out of the fridge or the biscuit tin during the day. If you think that it is unfair to totally restrict biscuits, crisps and sweets, then offer them only after he has eaten his meal.
- Allow him to, and encourage him to, self-feed as much as possible. Provide foods that he can pick up in his hands and allow him to be messy and play with his food. Unobtrusively help with loading the spoon and letting him put it in his own mouth.
- Gradually introduce small amounts of slightly more textured foods in the context of a more puréed meal so that he learns to cope with the new textures in his mouth. Encouraging self-feeding also helps him to be aware of the texture that is about to go into his mouth.
- If your child is ill, don't worry about appetite, just provide easy-to-eat foods and lots of drinks that he likes and wait until the illness is over. His appetite will miraculously return when he feels well again.

Television, toys and mealtimes

I wonder how many young children in Britain today sit and eat their meals in front of the television. With televisions in the kitchen, and the lack of space for dinner tables in many homes, we are developing a culture of eating on our laps in front of the TV. Having discussed distraction as a useful strategy for managing your young child in Chapter 3, it is obvious why many parents start to use the TV as a distraction if their child is having problems with eating. Hopefully you can pop a spoonful in his mouth while he is involved in his favourite video. The problem with this is that it is a short-term strategy that has no long-term gain. If your child is a reluctant eater, it is important to try and understand why he is reluctant.

- Are you having battles at meals if the TV is not on?
- Is he finding the quantity that you are giving too much?
- Are you too worried about the mess and so prefer to feed him while he is distracted rather than let him self-feed?
- Are you worried about the quantity that he eats and so prefer to feed him while he is distracted?
- Is it just a habit that has evolved?
- Will you have problems keeping him sitting still and paying attention if the TV is not on?
- Will he just run off and play if the TV is not on?

If the TV has become a method of control, of keeping your child in one place, this leads me to suppose than you cannot do it yourself. Is it best therefore to carry on with this rather precarious existence where you are dependent on the TV as a child minder/distracter? Or is it time to address the issue of child management and how to get your child to do what you want him to?

This pattern at mealtimes can lead to your child being spoon-fed by you for much longer than would normally be expected as he does not learn to do it himself. To eat by

himself he needs to concentrate on his food, look at it,
touch it and experience what it is and learn how to
manage the spoon. This requires focusing on the plate
rather than the TV or toys. Many children learn to self-
feed once the TV is switched off and the toys are put away.
Food then becomes something to enjoy rather than being
something that is put in their mouths and they don't really
know what it is. Have you ever tried the experience of
being fed while blindfolded by someone else? You
cannot see your food so you cannot anticipate what the
texture will be or guess what the taste will be. Allowing
your child to self-feed is a process of passing some of the
control to your child. He can start to choose what he will
and won't eat. Willpower comes into play and you have to
work out how best to manage the situation so that he eats a
good diet. You have to make a number of decisions about
what is important and how best to enable your child to eat
the foods that he needs.

- Does it matter if he eats with his fingers?
- Does it matter if he doesn't eat all of his vegetables?
- Does it matter if he spills some on the floor?
- Does it matter if he eats his chips dipped in chocolate
  pudding?
- Does it matter if he doesn't finish the whole plateful?
- Does it matter if he eats all of the meat before he eats
  the potato?
- Does it matter if he takes 35 minutes instead of 10
  minutes?

Hopefully none of these things should matter. If they do,
then why are you so bothered about it? What do you think
is going to happen that is so terrible? If he doesn't eat all of
his vegetables, have you another strategy for ensuring that
his vitamin C level is adequate? Does he have vitamin

drops? Does he eat some fruit? Think around the problem and find other solutions rather than getting stressed and into battles with food.

Staying at the table

If you do eat at the table, then sometimes it can be difficult to encourage toddlers to stay still long enough to have a meal. First make sure that he is at the correct height and able to reach. Sitting on an adult chair will not be sufficient; he is likely to need a booster seat to reach the correct height. Being comfortable is the first consideration. Secondly, toddlers have a very short concentration span and are unlikely to sit still if they have nothing to do. So don't call him to the table until his food is ready for him to eat.

Tim, aged 2 years, and his brother, John, aged 3 years, thought it was great fun to run around at mealtimes. They were able to run rings around their mother, who found that once she had caught one of them the other would wriggle away. This game was repeated at every meal with the boys deliberately being naughty. Their mother was exasperated and easily caught out by their antics. She was continually losing her temper and meals were becoming a huge problem for her. Part of the problem was her disorganisation in the kitchen. She did not have the food ready to involve them once they were at the table. She did not sit with them but tended to turn her back to get on with other jobs in the kitchen.

If your toddler thinks that it is fun to grab a handful of food and run off, then you need to make very clear what is not acceptable to you. Be prepared to catch him before he gets down, hook your foot behind the chair leg so that he can't push it out. He will need close physical monitoring from you to keep him there. You can develop a rule that says: if he wants to eat or drink, then he should do this only while sitting at the table. Food is not to be eaten on the run. This means that, if he has a snack, a packet of crisps, some sweets or a drink, then these should be given only while sitting at the table until he learns to sit still for meals.

Some parents get caught in the trap of following their toddler around the room with food. At some point, while their child is distracted by a toy, they pop a spoonful into their child's mouth and feel pleased that at least some food has gone in. This really is creating a rod for their own backs and is a short-term method that has no long-term gains. It is a much better game to sit at the table and encourage your toddler to come to you to get the food rather than you chasing him. The food is then used as a reward and gradually you can encourage him to sit down before he gets what he wants to eat. Don't let your desire to get some food into him dominate how you think and react. Use your head rather than your emotions.

My child is too fat

Many babies go through a very podgy stage at around 6 months of age; but once they start crawling and trying to walk you will find that the weight will drop off. The additional exercise they receive helps control their weight. It is important to have your baby regularly weighed by your health visitor at the baby clinic as they will help you monitor what is happening. Your baby's weight needs to be in keeping with his length or height.

If your child is overweight then think about your daily pattern and routine.

- Is he eating snacks and sugary drinks during the day? These can really overload a child who is also eating well at mealtimes. Change to water as the main drink, rather than squash or fizzy drinks.
- How much milk is he drinking during the day and night? The quantity of milk children need reduces when they are on solid foods as they can get calcium through cheese and yoghurts. Your child may still be drinking a couple of pints of milk a day. You could change to semi-skimmed milk to reduce the fat content, or just cut down to 1 pint. Your child may be drinking a lot of milk if he is attached to his bottle. The extra he has at night can make a considerable difference to his total calorie intake over 24 hours. If you are using the bottle at night as an aid to sleeping, then read the next chapter.
- Can he help himself to biscuits and sweets or can he open the fridge door and help himself? Sometimes it is difficult to know how much your child is eating if he helps himself. You may need to lock away the biscuit tin or even put a lock on the fridge door. If this is not possible then do not buy the sweet and high-calorie foods that he is eating. Leave out fruit that he can help himself to instead.
- Do you tend to give him something to eat to keep him quiet? It is easy to offer a snack or a drink if your child is being demanding or noisy. Watch out if you are using food as a pacifier.
- Do you think deep down that a fat child is healthy one? This is an old wives' tale and does not hold true in

modern-day society where nutritional levels are gen-erally very good. A fat child is an unhealthy one, and you may be laying down some health problems for him later in life.

- Does he have much exercise? Does he spend a lot of time sitting and watching TV? Is his physical activity limited by the size of your flat or house? Young children do need to get out each day, whatever the weather, and have a good run around. A visit to the park or a walk without the buggy and without being carried are essential for his health and well-being. Toddler gyms are around, playgroups have large activity toys, and even going to the local swimming pool for a splash around can be a great exercise in the winter if you don't want to walk in the rain. Make sure you only have the TV/video on for a limited amount of time each day, and try to have friends to play as he is bound to be active with them.

- Are you or your partner overweight? Being over weight often runs in families. This is not due to genetic traits but to social patterns of eating. Over-weight adults often have overweight pets, so it is clearly not genetic. You will impose your style of eating on your child. Your portions will be bigger, and you take pride in seeing your family eat up a large meal. Food will be used as a comforter, a pacifier, a reward and a celebration. You probably eat a high-fat and high-sugar diet with a lot of carbohydrates. You probably have a lot of snacks in the house. You may not take much exercise and so your child will also learn not to exercise. So think carefully about your own lifestyle and eating habits.

We are in the age of snack and ready-prepared foods, and for the most part they are fattening high-fat and high-sugar foods. They are very addictive, which we all know, and so it is very easy to lapse into having a quick fix on these when we are hungry. If you leave out crisps, biscuits and sweets next to fruit, which do you think your child will choose to eat? Children will not necessarily choose the correct diet for themselves, if left to their own choice, if these snack foods are available. If you are really serious about your child's weight, then just do not buy them or have them in the house.

> *Ahmed, aged 3 years, was overweight due to drinking three pints of milk a day out of his bottle as well as eating well. His mother was convinced that he needed milk in order to grow and did not realise that most of his nutrition was coming from his meals. He was very attached to his bottle and would demand it regularly throughout the day and night. His mother was unable to resist his demands as he would scream and hit her if she refused to give him his bottle. She began to water down his milk gradually so that the quantity of milk he was drinking was reduced. He gradually became less interested in his bottle as the taste changed and she was able to avoid a confrontation with him.*

It is generally unwise to put your child on a diet and expect him to lose weight as we would as adults. The best approach seems to be to control his eating to a static level and let him grow through the weight he has put on. Reducing his dependence on fatty snacks and sugary drinks will help this. Increasing his level of exercise is an essential part of weight control. Given the opportunity, most toddlers will be active and enjoy physical games. Take some time out to walk to the shops or to school to collect your other children, rather than always taking the car. If you can, ensure that you go out and expect your child to walk for at least half an hour every day. Riding a trike, going swimming or playing football are both great ways of increasing the amount of exercise and having fun at the same time. Toddler gyms, dance classes, the local children's playground, playgroups with a good open play area will all encourage your child to be more active.

Make sure that you do not take crisps, sweets and drinks out with you when you go shopping to keep him quiet in the buggy. Use books or toys instead, or make him walk and help you choose what to buy. If he demands a snack, then offer fruit. If he turns that down, then you know he is not really hungry and can wait for his meal.

Anna, aged 3 years, was very overweight and her GP was worried that her weight was affecting her health. Her mother was quite slim and could not explain why her daughter was so overweight. Observation of Anna's eating revealed that she did not eat excessively large meals but gradually her mother was able to reveal that she was having major marital problems and, every time she and her husband argued, she would give Anna a packet of biscuits to keep her quiet and out of the way in her bedroom. Anna was eating a tremendous amount of snack food in this way as her mother did not want her to witness the anger and violence.

Topical tips

- Wait until the end of the meal before you wipe your child's face and hands.

- Don't fight over control of the spoon.

- Your child is not rejecting you if he rejects your meal.

- 3-year-olds cannot design a menu.

- Your job is to keep the range of food options open.

- Keep calm and relaxed at mealtimes.

- Restrict snacks and milky drinks between meals to increase your child's appetite.

- Encourage self-feeding as soon as possible.

- Don't let your desire to get food into your child dominate how you think and react.

7

Sleeping and your child

Sleep problems are a very high priority for many parents. About one-quarter of parents of under-5s have children with disturbed sleep patterns, so you are not alone. If your sleep is continually disrupted, you can lose your patience and your sense of humour, and you become fractious and irritable. You may even dread going to bed at night, as you know that you are going to be woken within an hour or so of falling asleep and it feels like torture. Many parents seek sedatives from their GP for their toddlers in order to get some rest; but you may feel unhappy about giving medication for this type of problem and want to sort out the best way of managing it (Stores, 1996).

Sleeping and feeding

It is very easy to fall into the trap of using breast- or bottle-feeding as the method to get your baby to fall asleep. Babies do feel full and sleepy after a feed and so it is understandable; but beware that this does not become your main method of settling your baby, otherwise you will be setting up a problem for the future. Sucking is a pacifier and reduces the baby's level of responsiveness to his surroundings. Parents who rely on this can find that by about 10 months of age their infant may not be able to fall asleep without sucking, and if he finishes the feed before he has fallen asleep, what can they do? They also become trapped into providing a feed every time their baby wakes at night, as this is the only way to encourage settling to sleep again. Would you want this pattern to carry on into your toddler's second and third years? Don't forget that, if you are demand breast-feeding, it is you that will have to get up each time.

A simple and helpful routine is to change your baby's nappy after a feed so that he wakes up a little and then is put down to sleep feeling full and clean but slightly awake. He then learns to fall asleep without sucking, and this will help him, as he grows older, just to fall asleep at bedtime without needing you there.

It is easy for feeding and falling asleep to become muddled together and the first step in any plan to change your child's sleeping pattern is to think about how he falls asleep.

- Does he need you there while he falls asleep?
- Does he need to suck on a bottle/dummy or breast to fall asleep?
- Does he need rocking, stroking or cuddling while he falls asleep?

If your toddler needs you there at bedtime to fall asleep then it is highly likely that when he wakes in the night he will cry until you go to him and help him fall asleep again.

The pattern that you establish at bedtime will be repeated many times in the middle of the night. The dependence on sucking is part of this and will need to stop in order for you to have some peace (France & Hudson, 1993).

My child won't go to bed

Some toddlers refuse to go to bed, as they don't want to miss out on what is happening downstairs. If they are put to bed, they scream and cry until they are taken out again, or they get out by themselves and go back to where you are. Some parents have described putting their child back to bed 15–20 times in an evening. No wonder they give up and pretend their child has not arrived back in the room, or just let him fall asleep on the sofa. Other parents find that they have to lie down with their child in order for him to fall asleep. This can sometimes take an hour or more and they may find that they fall asleep themselves and miss their evening.

Parents will do anything to get their child to sleep. These are all examples of strategies parents have told me about:

- Going for a drive in the car.
- Banging a drum.
- Switching on the hoover or the washing machine.
- Musical toys.
- Musical tapes.
- Leaving lights on/off, doors open/closed, curtains open/closed.
- Rocking on lap or in pram or rocker.
- Pushing back and forwards in buggy.

No parent wants to hear their child cry at bedtime. It can feel very distressing and makes you question whether you are doing the right thing. You lose your confidence in what you want to achieve as you try to pacify the crying. It is important to keep sight of your aims. If you feel that having an evening to yourself is important for your own sanity, then you do need to work out how to get your child to go to bed and stay there (Wolfson, 1998).

- Your first decision is: What time should he go to bed? What time does he generally fall asleep now? If he mostly settles by 9 p.m., then choose this as his bedtime initially, you can always move it earlier once he learns the pattern of behaviour that is expected.
- Develop a bedtime routine that includes a bath/wash, changing, drink, story and a kiss or cuddle for the half-hour before his bedtime. This sets the scene for falling asleep in bed. Don't be tempted to get your child ready for bed and then let them come down and play for a while until he is tired, this is giving the wrong message. The bedtime routine needs to be consistent and predictable so that your child learns to associate it with going to bed. If he tends to fall asleep sucking on a bottle, give the drink earlier in the routine so that he is put to bed without the bottle. Sometimes offering a beaker rather than a bottle will help this transition.
- Put him in to his bed and then indicate that it is time to go to sleep by putting out lights and reducing contact with him.

There are now two routes you can take: letting him cry or gradual separation.

Letting him cry

If you are able to tolerate him crying then leave the room and wait for him to settle on his own. If he doesn't settle after 10 minutes then look in to see he is all right, tell him to go to sleep and then leave the room again. You can keep checking every 5–10 minutes, if you feel that you need to, but don't offer drinks, cuddles or kisses. This checking is really more for your benefit than your child's and, if you can manage not to go in, your child will learn to settle faster. Be clear that you want him to go to sleep and walk away. You can continue this until your child falls asleep by himself. But be warned, if you give in and start to cuddle or feed him after he has been crying, then you have very effectively taught him to cry for that length of time before he gets his own way. Some parents do not realise that giving in after a period of crying can make the problem much worse. Sadly, they end up trying this method, doing it wrongly and having a child who can cry for one-and-a-half hours or more at bedtime. So if you do plan to use this approach, you must ensure that your child falls asleep without you there at the end of it.

This approach is extremely effective and works quite rapidly. If he cries for half an hour the first night, this is likely to be down to 10 minutes the second night, and the third night to just a few minutes. Within three to four nights even the most difficult child will have learned to fall asleep without crying, as he has learned that there is no point in crying.

Some toddlers feel very cross that they are not in control and try even harder to get you to go in once they realise that the pattern is changing. Some scream much louder than you have ever heard before in temper, others change the pitch of their cry, some stop and start, others might cough and sound as if they are gagging or in the worst times they might vomit. These are all very effective strategies at getting you back in the room. If your child does vomit then just clear him up, change his clothes and put him back to bed calmly but firmly without any fuss. Keep in mind your end goal and stick to your decision.

If your toddler is in a bed and has learned to get out of his room then you need to think carefully about how to keep him in there. Each time he comes out of his room he is winning a bit of the game and it encourages him to keep on doing it. You can keep on taking him back but you should not give him any cuddles and you should be detached and not very pleased with him. Putting him straight back to bed may result in him getting out again. It can be quite hard to keep your temper if he is being deliberately insistent. Repeatedly putting him back will eventually teach him the lesson, but it can be exhausting and most parents will give up after three or four attempts. You really want to stop him coming out of his room in the first place, so you could put a stair gate across the doorway or you could temporarily lock the bedroom door until he falls asleep and then open it. This may result in him getting out of bed and falling asleep on the floor in his bedroom for a couple of nights, but you can always pick him up later and put him into bed or even just cover him up on the floor if you are worried about disturbing him. Once he realises that he cannot get out, he will stop getting out of bed.

Steve, at 18 months, would only fall asleep in his pram and his mother was worried that he had out-grown it and she did not know what she was going to do as he refused to go into a cot. She eventually decided to make a clean break of the pram and put it in the garage so that he could not see it. She then decided to leave him to cry in his cot until he fell asleep, as she wanted to teach him the new pattern as rapidly as possible. She initially sat beside his cot in order to comfort him but found that he was losing his temper with her and screaming at her, so she left the room and let him cry until he fell asleep. The first night he cried for nearly an hour, off and on; but the second night he only cried for 5 minutes and the third night he did not cry and settled to sleep with no problem.

Gradual separation

If you know that you will give in as soon as you hear your child cry then the above method will not work for you. Gradual separation is an alternative method that takes longer and requires more effort, but can be just as effective. The end goal is the same but the method of getting there is gentler and should not involve any crying.

The number of stages of separation that you go through will depend on you and your child. If at present you or your partner has to lie down in bed cuddling him so that he falls asleep, you need to devise a plan of gradually moving away from him, over successive nights, so that eventually he learns to fall asleep on his own without you being there. As you can see this can take 4–5 steps or up to 20 steps depending on how much separation you think you can teach him at each stage. Each step should take 2–3 nights before your child learns to accept this new regime. He may object on the first night of each new stage but will come to accept it if he feels secure that you will not leave him before he falls asleep. Once you reach a new stage of separation, don't go back to a previous stage if possible. The stages could be:

- Lie down on top of the covers, not in the bed with him.
- Lie down beside him but don't cuddle him.
- Sit on the bed rather than lie down.
- Sit on the bed and do not touch him.
- Sit on a chair beside the bed.
- Sit on a chair a few feet away from the bed.
- Sit on a chair out of sight in the room.
- Sit in the doorway.
- Sit outside the door and out of sight.
- Sit in your own bedroom.

The aim of reducing contact should also include your emotional reactions to him while he falls asleep. You need to be detached, cool and calm. Don't get involved in conversation, reassuring noises, songs or games of peek-a-boo. Your child will try hard to keep you looking at him, smiling and he may even start pulling faces to get a reaction from you. It is far better if you can try to ignore him. Don't make eye contact, look away, read a book or just close your eyes. The message should be that you just want him to go to sleep.

Marie would spend an hour each night pushing her 2-year-old backwards and forwards in his buggy in the bedroom in order to get him to fall asleep. The movement was a strong and violent to and fro move-

ment, which was wearing tracks in the carpet. She was feeling exhausted and did not know how to get out of the habit that had developed.

She agreed to use a plan of gradual change in which she successively reduced the distance she pushed him and reduced the violence of the movement. After two weeks he was able to fall asleep in his buggy without being pushed. We then agreed a plan for him to fall asleep in his bed rather than buggy, by initially cuddling him in his bed and then gradually reducing contact. It took her three months to teach him to fall asleep without her presence and, although it took a long time, she was delighted with the change.

Rewarding good behaviour

If your toddler is over three years of age, he will be able to understand the idea of getting a reward. You can tell him that you want him to stay in his bed or his bedroom once you have said goodnight and, if he doesn't come out, then he will get a little surprise present in the morning. This can work if your child already can stay in his room for some nights but not all. It means that he has a possibility of earning a reward. The present should be very small, e.g. collectors cards, a crayon or a sticker on a chart. When you give it to him in the morning do make a great fuss of what a clever boy he has been and how proud you are of him.

My child wakes me at night

You need your sleep in order to cope with the demands of the day, so don't feel guilty about wanting to sleep. Uninterrupted sleep is so important, and exhaustion is a destructive feeling that can undermine your relationship with all of the members of your family. You may have learned to exist on four or five hours of sleep, but you are not functioning at your best, and your patience and resilience will be limited. But it is important to get together with your partner and try to work out a plan that you both accept and will try and work on together. If one of you wants the child kept quiet in order to sleep, then the other partner is forced into a difficult situation where anything is done to keep the child quiet. You have also probably evolved a pattern of managing your child at night without really thinking of the long-term consequences. Taking him into your bed may have been fine when he was 1 year old, but is a different matter when it has been going on for three years and you find that your 4-year-old is taking up most of the space, kicking you, or that suddenly your second child is wanting to come into your bed as well (Douglas & Richman, 1984).

Letting him cry

Most children who wake at night have a problem with falling asleep on their own at bedtime. So your first step is to think about your bedtime routine and teach your child to fall asleep without your presence. In some cases this will solve the night-time problem immediately, while in others you also need to try the same methods in the middle of the night. If you have left him to cry at bedtime then you can do the same thing in the middle of the night. You may need to warn your neighbours and your other children that there may be some noise for a few nights. If you are exhausted, then perhaps you and your partner could take turns in being responsible on alternate nights. At least you can then put your head under the pillow and pretend it is nothing to do with you.

Gradual separation

If you have used gradual separation at bedtime, then you can do the same in the middle of the night. You may feel chilly at night if you are sitting up, so have a warm dressing-gown and slippers and see if you can put a comfortable chair in your child's room or have a large cushion on the floor to sit on; but try not to doze off.

Stopping drinks at night

Night waking is often maintained by having drinks and bottles, so if you find that you are automatically offering a drink when your child wakes you should reconsider this. If you are really worried about thirst then offer water but don't go to the effort of warming up some milk. I would guess if you offer your child water you might have it thrown back at you, but at least you know he is not thirsty.

Changing this pattern of having bottles can be managed rapidly or slowly. You can throw the bottles away or refuse to give the expected juice or milk, but you will have to face the consequences of your child's objections. If you can let him cry it out and not give in, then he will learn quickly. Putting the bottles in the bin on the day that the rubbish is collected, in the sight of your child, will indicate to him that your decision is final. This helps your willpower that evening when he demands the bottle, which you no longer have.

If you cannot face the crying, you can use a more gradual method of change. Watering the milk down over successive nights will change its taste and your child will eventually stop drinking it and indicate that it is not what he wants. At that point you need to make a clear decision that you will not increase the milk content but sit out the problem until your child stops complaining.

The greatest problem is often your own anxiety that your child will not be able to fall asleep without the bottle. You need to develop confidence that your child will learn to fall asleep without sucking if you can stand up to a few disturbed nights. Given that you are already getting up to warm up the milk, in reality it should not be much worse than it is at present; and eventually it will be much better. Your own sense of guilt and uncertainty undermines your ability to make a decision about what to do, so try to work out why you have found it so hard to change this pattern until now. Reassure yourself that he does not need the nutrition at night as he eats well during the day; if he's thirsty he can drink water, so you are not depriving him.

Timmy, a 3-year-old, was drinking up to 2 pints of milk during the night from his bottle. He woke his mother about four times a night and she would have to warm the milk before he would drink it. He could only fall asleep while sucking on the bottle, and when she had tried to stop using it, he had become very angry and screamed. Her husband had told her to carry on with the bottle so that he could get some sleep. She needed a plan to stop using the bottle which her husband would agree to. They discussed the problem and both decided to throw the bottles away at the beginning of a holiday so that father's ability to cope at work would not be affected by Timmy's crying. Timmy began to sleep through without waking after four nights without his bottles.

Rewards for not disturbing you at night

You can also use a reward chart or a little surprise in the morning for not being woken. Do tell your child about this plan and try to make him keen and excited about the possibility of earning a reward. You both will benefit if he is successful.

I had one instance where a 3-year-old girl was earning stickers for staying in her own bed all night, and she realised that she could still earn the sticker if she stayed in bed and called out to her parents to come and see her. They then had to change their agreement to include not being woken up by her before she earned the sticker. So beware! Your child can be a very rapid learner when he wants to get his own way.

Stop your child coming into your bed

You have probably allowed your child into your bed as a short-term measure to gain some sleep, but have found that it has carried on longer than you want. You may now be ready to encourage him to sleep in his own bed. There is no reason to feel guilty that you want your bed to yourselves; it is just a process of teaching your child what is he is supposed to do. Of course he is going to prefer to sleep with you. So you will need to teach him to unlearn a pattern that has existed for some time and also go against his will.

If he is still in a cot, then your life is easier as your child is not able to get out and come into your room by himself. You will need to decide together that from a certain night you will no longer allow your child into your bed at night, and then stick to your decision. Once this is agreed, you need to choose how best to manage your child in his own cot: whether you leave him to cry or use a gradual separation approach is up to you. It is imperative that during this learning time you never take him into your bed, even for a 5-minute cuddle. He will then learn the new pattern much faster. If you find yourself feeling sorry for him, or guilty, then just think about your long-term goal. It will be best for all of you in the long run, and the sooner he learns the new pattern the better. This process of learning will not hurt him and he will not feel rejected, he is just trying to get his own way.

If your child is in a bed, then it is likely that he is coming in by himself during the night and creeping into your bed. You may not even be aware that he is coming in and just wake up to find him there.

Mia, aged four, would creep into her parent's bed at night and crawl up between them under the duvet from the bottom of the bed. Her parents would wake up to find her sprawled across the middle with both of them clinging onto the edges of the bed trying not to disturb her. They decided that they had had enough and wanted her to stay in her own room.

They tried tucking in a bedcover at the bottom of the bed so that she could not get into it easily. But this did not work. They then closed their bedroom door so that they would hear her coming in. But she learned to be very quiet. They did not want to lock their bedroom door, as they did not want her wandering around the house at night, nor did they want to lock her bedroom door. Eventually they decided on a reward programme for not coming in, combined with hanging a wind chime from the ceiling so that, as their door opened, it struck the chime and they woke up. Within three nights Mia had learned not to go into her parent's bed, as each time she tried they woke and made her go back to her own room. On the night that she did not go in, she earned some sparkly stickers in the morning. She was delighted with her reward and did not seem at all distressed about not sleeping in her parent's bed.

The main rule is not to allow your child into your bed, even for a few minutes. If he comes in, you must either tell him to go back to his bed, or take him back, with no extra cuddles or kisses. For the first couple of nights you may have to get up several times to take him back, if he is insistent; and you may feel that the whole process is worse than letting him in. But don't give in. A reward programme helps as a great incentive for him to stay in his own bed all night, so it is worth combining this with your new restriction.

If your child is very strong-willed and this is not working, you may need to think about a physical barrier rather than just a psychological barrier. Closing his bedroom door, putting a stair gate across his doorway or even locking his door for one night may be enough for him to learn that, if he comes out more than once, that you will carry out your plan. Usually you only need to do this once for him to learn that you mean what you say.

Stopping your child calling out

Some children learn that you will come if they call out to you with a reason for your attention. This can vary from having an itchy knee, to wanting the curtains properly closed; they may have a stuffy nose or they need to go to the toilet. The list can be very long, and if you write down all of the excuses, you will soon see that this is just a manipulation that you are falling for. The basic requests for a drink or toilet can be managed relatively easily. Always leave a drink of water in a teacher beaker in easy reach of your child so that he can help himself at night. He will not need a fill-up during the night. If he needs the toilet then he can either go by himself, if he is old enough, or leave a potty in his room so that he can go by himself. If he is in nappies, then just ignore him. The period of toilet training for night-time dryness is a little tricky, and you may just have to accept a few broken nights around this time; but once this is over it should not be accepted as a regular excuse. The other excuses can be ignored. Your child may be feel very indignant and you may feel, 'If just moving the curtain a bit will help her sleep, why shouldn't I do it?' Then think how long this has been going on for and the list of other 'little' requests that have kept you going in and out several times each night. Again, a reward programme for not calling out to you can help the change process speed up.

My child gets up too early

Getting up too early is a particularly difficult pattern to change, as your child has already had all of the sleep he needs for the night, and may be up and bouncing around ready to face the day at 5 a.m. Sometimes a change of nappy and drink at this time will encourage him to settle down for another hour of sleep, if he has been wet or hungry. How many of us take our children into our beds at this time in the hope of getting an extra little sleep but find that they are climbing all over us and poking our eyes to get us to wake up? You normally don't achieve any more rest, so you may as well get up.

A 3-year-old may be able to learn to delay coming in to wake you up if provided with an incentive or reward for waiting until his side light goes on at 6 a.m. before he comes out of his room. Time switches for lights or radios can be very helpful in this type of problem as they provide a cue to the child, who cannot tell the time, when they are allowed to get up.

The other way of coping is to take turns with your partner about who gets up and leaves the other to have some extra sleep until 7 a.m. At least you can look forward to your 'lie in' morning. I am sure that the TV or video is often used as a babysitter in the early morning, but it is really unwise and dangerous to have a preschooler up wandering around the house while parents are still tucked up in bed trying to get a bit more sleep.

What is so maddening is that your toddler is able to go back to bed at 10 a.m. for a nap, while you have to get on with your work.

Nightmares and night terrors

Some children have disturbed sleep due to nightmares or night terrors and this can equally disturb your sleep. Nightmares are bad dreams that occur during the light phase of sleep (rapid-eye-movement sleep), and we have all experienced them. Once children can talk they are able to describe that they are having bad dreams from about the age of 2 years. This age also coincides with a surge in the frequency of nightmares that may be linked to the great developmental changes that are occurring at this time. Some nightmares are about specific situations like witches, crocodiles or nasty people. Others may be about being chased, being hurt or falling. But the main feature is that your child wakes up feeling frightened and can re-member what happened in his dream. He needs reassur-ance and a cuddle and will often go back to sleep with no problem. Nightmares are often triggered by something that happened in the day, events in a story or something seen on television.

Night terrors are very different from these and occur during deep sleep. Your child may sweat and thrash around in bed or scream. He may have his eyes open and may be waving his arms around, but he is not awake. In the morning he will have no memory of the episode, although you do. It is difficult to wake your child up when he is in this state, so it is best just to sit with him until he calms down. It is not a sign of any deep psychological disturbance or fear. Don't get worried about it. He will settle again after 5–15 minutes and will know nothing about it. This phase will be over quite rapidly but may re-emerge at different points for short periods, as he grows older. If you are really concerned about it and it is disturbing the household severely, then

watch out for the restlessness that is often the starting
point for the night terrors. As soon as your child starts
to show signs of sweating or moving, then wake him up
and disturb the sleep rhythm so that he doesn't drop into
the deep sleep phase. This can often prevent the night
terror from occurring, but it means that you need to be
very aware of the pattern of his sleeping, and you still have
to get up.

Topical tips

- Encourage your baby to fall asleep without sucking on the breast or bottle after 6 months of age.

- Think about who is in charge at night, you or your child.

- Develop a bedtime routine with a clear end-point.

- Children can force themselves to stay awake after the age of 10 months and can suffer from insufficient sleep.

- Think about what your child is gaining from waking at night.

- Ensure that your child falls asleep without you present if you are letting him cry.

- Stop giving drinks and cuddles in the middle of the night if you want uninterrupted sleep.

- Be consistent in your reactions so that your child learns faster.

- Become emotionally detached and ignore your child if you sit with him while he falls asleep.

- Take turns on alternate nights to ensure that you each get some rest.

8

Fears and worries

It may seem strange to think about toddlers as having fears and worries, but when you consider how strange the world is and how unpredictable it can be to a young child, then these fall into the normal range of experience. Loud noises, strangers, being left alone, feeling uncertain and vulnerable, big dogs, insects, masks and clowns can all frighten young children. I am sure that you can add more.

Your child will look for your reaction to a situation when he is feeling uncertain. It is as if he is checking out whether he should be frightened or not. Strange or unfamiliar settings, strangers, strange toys to play with will all create uncertainty and your child will want to check out with your expression whether they are safe or not. You can already see how your reaction will influence how your child learns to react. If you are a worrier, over-protective or generally anxious, then your child will pick up these cues and could start to show similar patterns of anxiety. This interaction between you could start to encourage dependency rather than autonomy and self-confidence in your child.

Children have very different temperaments from birth and some are more naturally cautious and anxious than others. They find change difficult, they overreact to loud noises, they may need more pacifying in terms of sucking in order to calm down, and they find separation from their mothers more difficult. It seems as if they become aroused by events around them more easily than other children and they need help in order to modulate their reaction to the world.

Patterns of behaviour from this young age do have an effect on how we behave as we grow older. Children who are active and outward-going tend to be like that as adolescents, while children who are timid, fearful and anxious also tend to continue to show those features when they are older.

My child is a worrier

Katie, aged three, was described as very fearful by her mother. She hated loud noises and would make her mother go a long way round to the shops to avoid some road works on their road. She would cry in the house when the vacuum cleaner was switched on, and so her mother cleaned when she was asleep. She would startle and cry if she heard a dog bark and so was reluctant to go to the park. Even at playgroup she would sit with her hands over her ears, as she did not like the noise that the children were making. She had started to resist going to playgroup because she did not like the unpredictable noise if another child cried. Her mother had tried to avoid situations that would upset her and had stopped the playgroup attendance, but was concerned that Katie was becoming cut off from her own age group.

The avoidance was making the situation worse, so a plan was made to help Katie gradually learn to cope with the noises. Her mother took her gradually closer to the road works on successive days until she was able to go past it with no problem. She used the vacuum cleaner in another room and gradually brought it closer to Katie in the house until she could be in the same room. At playgroup she was encouraged to stay initially for a short time and then the time was extended until she learned to cope with the whole morning. Katie became much more confident and able to play with her friends without being fearful and avoidant.

When your child is showing anxiety and fear it is natural to want to protect him and take him away from the problem situation. But if you find that your child's ability to carry on a normal social life is being affected by his fears, then he needs help to learn how to cope better rather than avoid the problem. Your job as a parent is to control the impact that the world has on your child. You modulate and control his experiences and help him learn how best to manage new or fearful situations. If a child is anxious, it will not help to force him to face up to his fears. This can often make the situation worse if the child cannot control his level of anxiety. Toughening him up by throwing him in the deep end can be very traumatic. It seems far better to gradually introduce him to the feared situation with your support and reassurance. This is a process of desensitisation and is a technique that is used with adults who are phobic. If you are frightened of spiders, imagine how you would feel if you were forced to pick up a tarantula. You would feel terrified and traumatised. But if you were helped to touch, with a tissue, a tiny spider that was light in colour, that was not moving and that did not have black hairy legs you might feel able to cope and you would have taken the first step on the road to learning to overcome your phobia. So think about how you can help your child gradually face up to his fears, and how your emotional reaction when he is distressed may be compounding the problem.

Phobias are often linked to a specific experience that your child has had. Being frightened by a barking dog, being stung by a wasp, hearing a story or watching a TV programme can all be the cause of a phobia developing. Something that seemed trivial to you may have seemed terrible to your child. In other cases your phobias may be transferred to your child. If you're terrified of spiders, then your reaction when you see one will alarm your toddler and he may learn to be frightened because you are.

Sam, aged three, was terrified of having his hair washed or going in the bath. His mother suspected that he had become worried after a child minder had let him go under the water in the bath at the age of 18 months. He had panicked and since that time refused to bath.

We developed a plan of desensitising Sam's fear by encouraging him initially to stand in the bath with no water in it while his teeth were cleaned every morning and night. One inch of warm water was then added to the bath and he was encouraged to

> *stand in it on a non-slip mat. Toys were put in the bath and he was encouraged to crouch down and play with them. Gradually the level of the water in the bath was increased up to 4 inches and he was encouraged to splash and be washed without necessarily sitting down. After about 1 month he had learned to sit down in the water and his mother was able to wash his hair with the shower attachment to the tap.*

Ways to help your child overcome fears and phobias include:

- Accept and understand your child's fear. Do not make fun or ridicule him.
- Reassure and calm your child and try a gentle and gradual approach to the feared object.
- Don't force contact with the feared object or you may induce a panic.
- Use immediate and simple rewards to increase your child's motivation to approach the feared object in stages.
- Set the goals of change as small manageable steps. Don't rush it.

Sometimes avoidance or reluctance to cooperate is interpreted as fear and shyness when in fact it is just a control issue.

> *Michael, aged 4, refused to have his hair cut and said he was frightened of going to the hairdressers. He also refused to have his nails cut and was*

described by his mother as very shy in new situations.
She thought these were phobic reactions and that he
needed help with his anxiety. In fact it was more of a
compliance problem. He generally liked to have his
own way and did not enjoy situations where others
had control over him. His cooperation improved with
a reward programme for doing what his mother
wanted, and she realised that he had not been
really frightened.

My child is timid and shy

Shyness is one way in which your child tries to regulate
the impact of events on himself. Hiding his face in your
lap, hiding behind people, not making eye contact and not
smiling can be the result of anxiety in social settings.
Some children take some time to warm up to new settings
and new people: they observe for a while before joining in.
Often, if left alone, they will gradually come closer and
want to join in, if not forced. Their interest in the activity
is often one way of overcoming their social shyness.

If your child is shy with other children, then having
one particular child to play over and over again will enable
your child to feel familiar and more confident. Relating to
one other is much easier than relating to a whole group. So
help him cope with the transition to playgroup by learning
to play with one or two other children first.

Shyness can also become a bit of a habit, particularly
when great efforts are made to involve the shy child. It
seems that the more effort you make the less the child

tries. So be careful not to give too much attention to his avoidant behaviour.

Comfort habits

Holding, sniffing, rubbing and sucking a security blanket, a dummy, a special teddy or a piece of mum's clothing are different ways in which children comfort themselves. It is interesting how parents often enjoy seeing their child show an attachment to a particular cuddly toy and will often encourage the child to have one to go to bed with. Even from the age of 6 months parents will put a special toy next to their child in bed as he falls asleep – although I have also known 3-year-olds who demand to take each of their soft toys in turn to bed so that the others don't get jealous.

I am sure you have heard of many stories of mothers having problems washing their child's security blanket because their toddler cannot manage without it, and it would spoil the smell of it. So we see young children walking around clutching grubby bits of cloth or soft toys. It can be helpful to encourage attachment to two blankets or toys in order to overcome this problem and make it possible to wash one while your child has the other. This is a very normal phase of behaviour and does not indicate that your child is particularly anxious. But as your child becomes older it can sometimes be awkward, and starts to be embarrassing for the child if he can't go for a sleep-over at a friend's house without his 'blanket'. In many situations the blanket or toy gradually falls apart with the heavy use and your child becomes accustomed to a smaller and more frayed piece of the original. This natural reduction in size is a very effective way of gradually coping without the 'comforter', as long as you don't try and replace it with a new one. Some 5-year-olds end up holding a few strands of their original blanket, which they sniff or rub contentedly. If the 'comforter' that your child has is durable and not diminishing in size, and he is still hauling around a complete cot blanket or a large soft toy at the age of four, then some judicious work with the scissors might be necessary to help it reduce in size over the course of a couple of months.

Of course, if you leave this precious object somewhere, or lose, it then it can cause a lot of distress. He may attach to another one, but usually, after a few nights, he will learn to cope without it and will learn or develop another comfort habit if he needs to.

Dummy-sucking and thumb-sucking are other ways in which children comfort themselves. In fact the Americans call dummies 'pacifiers'. A dummy can be a real problem at night if your child is dependent on it for falling asleep. Under-2s can be very distressed and need you to find their dummy for them in the middle of the night if it has fallen out of their mouths. Some parents manage this by having lots of dummies around all of the time so that their child is not dependent on only one. Having lots in the cot means that your toddler might be able to find one by himself at night without calling you to help.

There are many uneasy reactions from professionals and parents to children sucking dummies. It is important to consider why you are offering one to your baby. It really is not necessary, but I guess that parents who have babies that cry a lot use dummies as one way of gaining some peace and quiet as well as helping their baby calm down. Babies who are very fretful and unsettled may be helped, but it does set up a problem for the future when you want to remove it. The other problem is that a baby's cry is a communication and it may be important to try and work out what is the problem rather than stop the communication. This is when health professionals have become very wary of dummies. Seeing a young child walking around with a dummy in his mouth most of the day means that he is not communicating effectively, he is not learning to speak, and he may become more dependent on the dummy for comfort rather than going to their parents for a cuddle. In severe cases a dribble rash can develop around the mouth. I have also known children who have severe feeding problems and who are underweight depend on dummies as a way of avoiding food. As soon as they feel hungry they suck on a dummy instead of drinking or eating. So be careful that the dummy does not block communication. Let it be used, if necessary, as a comforter to fall asleep with; but try and prevent it being used during the day. You can teach your child that it is only for use in bed and not while walking around.

Of course thumbs and fingers are built-in, portable and not losable comforters, which are available at all times. Foetuses suck their thumbs in the womb, and babies can manage to get their own thumbs into their mouths by the age of 3–4 months. This will often offset the use of a dummy, unless you have introduced the dummy before this age for a crying baby. Thumb- or finger-sucking will occur at times of tiredness, boredom, and stress. It can also carry on into the teens. Many children stop this between the ages of 3 and 4 years, but a few will carry on and may need help in learning how to stop. It can be accompanied by hair-twirling and hair-sniffing, cloth-rubbing, rocking, humming, and a range of other self-comforting habits. It does help your child calm down, but can develop into a habit that invades large parts of the day. If it carries on into school age you may find that your child switches off in class while

thumb-sucking and misses some of what is being taught.
You can imagine that if you felt calm and peaceful and
preoccupied with a pleasurable feeling in a business
meeting, you would not concentrate particularly well,
although you may appear to be listening.

In general there is no real need to be concerned about
the effect of thumb-sucking on your child's teeth until
after the age of 6 years. But it does seem a good idea to
try and stop it before your child goes to school and is
exposed to a lot more stress than he will have experienced
at home. There have been many different ways of trying to
stop this highly self-reinforcing habit:

- Painting on a nasty flavour nail paint.
- Putting sticking plaster on the thumb.
- Wearing gloves.
- The dentist providing a palatal crib in the mouth.
- Reminding your child not to suck his thumb.
- Rewards for not sucking.
- Interrupting pleasurable activities if the child thumb-
  sucks, e.g. watching TV or listening to a story.
- Teaching your child to clench his hand around his
  thumb and count to 20.

It is important not to increase stress levels by shouting or
being angry about it. You don't want your child to become
a covert thumb-sucker – which may lead to more thumb-
sucking rather than less.

Rituals and repetitions

Can you remember not walking on the cracks in the pave-
ment, or touching every third railing as you went to

school? Young children develop these little rituals very easily. You may have to leave the door open a certain amount at night or kiss them three times before you say goodnight and then walk out backwards blowing kisses. They may need their toys in a certain position in their bedroom. In fact we encourage rituals in daily life by having routines that are predictable and remove the continual decision-making that is otherwise required. I bet you drive the same route to work each day, and park in the same place if you can. The problem comes when we cannot carry out our routine or ritual and we then become very anxious and worried. Rituals are rather like superstitious behaviour. We do it to ward off anxiety. As was mentioned above, some children are generally quite anxious and your job as parents is to try and help them cope with the worrying aspects of their world. So you accept certain rituals as ways of encouraging coping, particularly around falling asleep at night.

Sometimes these rituals can suddenly take on a life of their own and you are caught unawares by the fact that your child is feeling compelled to do them. You may feel that complying with his demands to do things in the same way is helpful; but if you meet a temper outburst because you have not done it exactly the way you should, then beware. Your child can start to be very controlling and in charge, which is not a healthy experience for him or for you. Bring in small changes that help him learn to cope with change, e.g. close the door one night because you have visitors and you don't want him disturbed, kiss him once or four times instead of three times or try to get him to guess how many times you are going to do it. You need to help him learn that an increase in his anxiety due to change is nothing to be worried about. Once he faces up to it and realises that nothing terrible happens, he will realise that the rituals are unnecessary.

Coping with being apart

Separation anxiety is one of the main fears that young children experience. From the age of about 9 months they can become more clingy and will not let you out of their sight. You find that you even have to take him into the bathroom with you, as he cannot tolerate you being behind a closed door even for a few minutes. This can be very wearing, as you have to have your baby with you every time you leave the room. Some babies become very attached to their dads for a period of time. Be careful that you do not feel left out if your baby is showing a closer attachment to one of you than to the other. It can and does change, and does not in any way mean that he prefers one of you more.

Once your child is mobile he will follow you around and hang onto you, or demand to be carried if you move too fast. Many parents find that, if they sit down quietly, their child will develop confidence to wander away and play, but that, if they are on the move doing jobs in the house, their child clings onto them and demands a lot of attention. If you can see it from your child's perspective, you can understand that when Mum is sitting down she is a safe base to explore from, but when she is moving around she needs to be watched and held onto in case she goes out of sight unpredictably.

Environmental change will increase your child's anxiety about separation. So if you move house, go to a strange house or go on holiday, you will find your child far more clinging than he may have been previously.

Teaching separation starts to become an important feature once a child is over the age of two as he may start to attend a playgroup. Prior to the big event it is helpful to teach your child more gradually how to tolerate brief separations from you while he is with familiar people. A close friend or relative can help out as you leave your child with them for gradually longer periods, assuring him that you will come back. If your child is particularly clingy this may take some time; but do persevere as he will learn to cope. It can be quite difficult for some children who are separated for the first time at playgroup or nursery. Most playgroups will allow you to stay while your child settles in and then encourage you to leave the room for ten minutes. A gradual transition period is helpful for both of you. But, when they leave their child at nursery on the first day of school, it is often the mothers who have the greater problem. Many mothers describe how they burst into tears when they get home as they feel it is the first major step of their baby growing away from them.

Suzie started half days at a local playgroup at age three but had great difficulties settling in. She would scream when her mother left her there, would be uncooperative and sulky with the play staff, and would be cross but clingy when her mother returned. After three weeks she was still not settling. Then it was pointed out that Suzie might be feeling jealous, as her mother always brought her new baby to nursery when she dropped Suzie off. She would see her mother showing the baby to everyone and then going home with him, leaving her alone at nursery. It was suggested that she leave her baby with a neighbour while she brought Suzie to playgroup and that she make it a special time for them to walk along together. Suzie found it much easier to settle after

> *this without seeing her mother leave with her rival in*
> *her arms.*

If you decide to go back to work during your baby's
first year it is vital for you to feel confident in your child's
care arrangements while you are apart. This separation
can feel very difficult and you will be understandably
ambivalent. From your baby's perspective it is probably
easier for the transfer of care to take place before he is 8
months of age rather than at the end of the first year when
he has become aware of strangers and shows stranger
anxiety. Your baby will probably adapt faster than you
will. Babies are designed to survive as long as they are
given the opportunity to have consistent and loving
care. The worst situation is when they are handed
around between strangers. They do not have time to
create meaningful or predictable relationships before
they are passed onto the next person. Transitory care
arrangements with multiple au pairs or child-minders
every few months is not ideal and should be avoided.
Aim for a more long-term arrangement if possible with
a child-minder, relative or nanny who will agree to care
for your child for at least a year. No arrangement ever feels
as comfortable as you caring for your own child, but safe-
guards such as observing the carer with your own or other
children, following up references and talking to other
parents who have used the child-minder will help you
make up your mind.

Topical tips

- Anxious children need help to cope with their fears rather than avoid them.

- Children can pick up anxiety from their parents.

- Desensitisation is more effective than confrontation.

- Comfort habits can develop into longer-term problems.

- Children develop rituals to ward off anxiety.

- Testing reality helps children realise that there is no need to be fearful.

- When Mum is sitting down she is a safe base to explore from.

- Teaching separation gradually will help your child when he starts nursery.

- Mothers often have more trouble parting than their children do on the first day of school.

9

Dry at last

Teaching toilet training

Toilet training used to be a really big issue for mothers in years gone by, but the advent of disposable nappies and automatic washing machines has removed the stress and strain of mountains of washing of dirty terry nappies. These days we seem much more able to wait until the child is 'ready' with the result that many children are toilet trained with the utmost of ease.

You will probably start thinking about this when your child is about 18 months old. This is the time when many children are able to hold onto their urine for a short period of time. You will know that the time is getting near when your child stays dry after nappy change for about an hour. This demonstrates that their bladder has some control. There is also a pressure from some nurseries that will not accept a child unless they are reliably toilet trained. Given that many children start nursery between the ages

of 2 and 3 years, this is probably going to be fine and is
nothing to worry about.

When you are ready to start teaching, buy a potty and
encourage your child to sit on at 'peak' times, just after a
meal, first thing in the morning or at bedtime. The first
few times you manage to catch a wee in the potty you
should be ecstatic so that your child realises what it is
that you want. Children often come into the bathroom
with you and watch while you go to the toilet; this is
all-important learning – although, when little girls try to
wee while standing up like Daddy, they need some rapid
correction. Sitting dolls and teddies on potties all helps
reinforce the idea – there are even dolls that wee, which
can be helpful. Once your child has managed to wee on
demand when on the potty a few times, then you can
seriously start toilet training and leave off nappies.

It is not unusual to go through a few days when your
child is 'potted' two or three times an hour. It is often
helpful to do this in summer when you can allow your
child to run around the garden without a nappy on and
with a potty in easy reach so that you can encourage frequent sit-downs. It is always so much more relaxing to be
on the grass than on your lounge carpet when you do this.

If you concentrate on a few days when you are not
likely to be going on long car journeys or out to the
shops, then you can concentrate the learning and hopefully succeed in a short time. If you do have to go and pick
up another child from school, then you will need to put a
nappy back on. But you can appreciate that, if your child
wets the nappy, then he is unlearning all that you have
tried to teach him.

As you gain success you will pass through a brief phase
of a couple of months when you carry a potty around with
you at all times for emergency stops. At least before the
advent of shopping centres you could hold your child over
the gutter in town if necessary! It is important to realise

that this is a time of muscle learning and, like learning to ride a bike, it takes some time. You getting upset and shouting will not speed up the process, and may even delay it if your child becomes anxious about your reaction. Think how difficult it is for you to wee when someone is hassling you, banging on the door, or listening.

The speed of learning to stay dry varies between children, and boys are generally a bit slower than girls in learning this control. Don't worry if your training does not appear to work. Leave it a couple more months and your child may be then sufficiently mature to learn. Approximately 60% of children are dry in the day by the age of two and a half, while 87% are dry by age three (Von Gontard, 1998).

Children who take longer than this to stay dry in the day usually have a family history of day wetting or enuresis. Genetic factors do have a part to play in the age at which dryness is achieved. Sometimes illness can delay learning and occasionally stress or anxiety can lead to lapses in control. Repeated lapses in control during the day may indicate a urinary tract infection. Irritation or burning feelings, a strange smell to the urine plus more frequent urination are usually indicators. Go to your GP to have it checked.

Your child will pass into a stage of being able to warn you that he needs the potty; but the time delay is very short initially, so you have to move very quickly. During this phase your child is still likely to wet while asleep and so you should keep putting on a nappy at night and for daytime naps. Make sure you dress your child in quick-release clothes to reduce the risk of accidents. But do take out a spare change of clothes for a couple of months during this unpredictable time. I have never been convinced about trainer pants because I am not too sure what the message is – is it all right to wee in them or not? I think that a child who knows he is in real pants seriously knows that he has to indicate when he wants to go to the toilet.

Even though your child may be able to indicate when he wants to go to the toilet, he may not be totally reliable, so watch out for tell-tale signs of hopping about a bit or holding himself, or just the length of time from when he went last time. This is a joint effort between you and him in order to avoid accidents and he needs your help and prompting. Even so, you may still experience the odd accident, which will either indicate that your child is sickening for something or that he was so preoccupied with what he was doing that he forgot. Excitement, fear and anxiety will also have an adverse effect at times. So if your child is having regular 'accidents' after he has been dry in the day, think carefully about what else is happening that might be upsetting him. Many children have wet themselves at nursery because they were too frightened to ask to go to the toilet, thought they didn't know where to go or were just shy.

Moving on to using the toilet rather than a potty is another sign of growing up. Some children make that decision for themselves. It is helpful to have a footstool available so that he can steady himself while sitting on the toilet rather than having feet dangling. Also, a children's toilet seat which sits on top of the ordinary one will stop him falling in.

Kevin was still wetting and soiling himself in the day at the age of 4 years. His parents had tried to toilet train him without success. He had been an ill baby and was quite underweight for his age and his bottom had little fat on it, so sitting on a potty was uncomfortable. He thought a potty was for babies and so refused to use it He had always avoided it and yet he was too small to manage the toilet and he was frightened of falling into it.

We devised a two-part plan. First was to encourage him to pass urine while standing up at the toilet. An incentive of earning a chocolate button every time he did a wee in the toilet standing up solved the problem within a couple of days. The problem of the discomfort and fear of sitting down on the toilet was solved by using a child's toilet seat padded with nappy inserts so that he felt safe and comfortable. A footstool gave him stability and he was encouraged to sit and look at a book while he did a poo. Within a couple of weeks the problem was all over and he felt more confident and his parents were greatly relieved.

Make sure that if your child goes to play at a friend's house that the words used for going to toilet are understandable. My older daughter reminded me when she said how strange it was when she went to a friend's house and her mother asked her if she 'wanted to spend a penny'. She hadn't a clue what this meant and remembers expecting to be given a penny.

It is possible to use a star or reward chart for children over three years of age to encourage consistent day dryness. You can use two routes:

1 To encourage having dry pants you should initially choose an easy length of time that your child could be dry, e.g. breakfast to lunchtime. Once he is predictably earning stars, then lengthen the time taken to earn one until he earns one for the whole day. The aim is not for your child to hold it in all day but to use the toilet appropriately when he needs to in order to stay dry.

2 To encourage going to the toilet your child can earn a star each time he passes urine in the toilet or potty. This does need monitoring and should not happen just on your child's report. You don't want to encourage twenty trips to the toilet in order to earn stars, so be careful about how you use this approach and see that it is achieving the right goal. Don't forget that the stars or stickers on chart are an important demonstration of your pleasure and praise at the progress your child is showing.

Keeping clean

Once your child learns to poo in a potty or on the toilet you will experience a great relief, as dirty nappies are much more unpleasant than wet ones. Usually bowel training is not a separate issue from bladder training; it seems to happen at the same time. Some children are very conscious of the fact that they have soiled their nappy and want changing immediately, but others can sit in it for hours. It is often possible to predict when the bowel movement is going to occur as they tend to be rather regular events if your child is well. So encouraging potty use at this time will increase the chance of success.

Some children become worried about passing a motion in the potty and ask for their nappy to be put back on so that they can relieve themselves.

Sarah's mother was worried as her 3-year-old refused to use the potty for bowel movements. She was a fastidious little girl and really disliked the smell, sight or knowledge of her motions. She would scream until her mother put a nappy on her for her to pass a motion, even though she had been dry in the day from the age of 18 months. Her mother thought that she had a 'complex' about it and did not know how to manage her. She would go and hide behind the sofa to pass a motion and then insist that her mother removed the nappy immediately.

She had no history of constipation or pain on passing motions; she had just learned to be very controlling of her mother, who had tried to stay calm, relaxed and cooperative with Sarah's demands. Sarah preferred to use the toilet rather than the potty and had a child's toilet seat to make it more comfortable for her. She sat on it happily enough to pass urine.

We decided that there was no reason not just to throw away her nappies and tell her that she could not have them again. A potty was placed behind the sofa where she could go to pass a motion if she wanted to, or she could go on the toilet. She was offered an incentive of a little surprise if she did pass a motion on the toilet, and her mother was prepared to sit with her and read her a story if she wanted it. Her mother stayed calm and supportive and helped her through her anxiety about not having her nappies available. Once she had passed one motion, the next day, there were no further problems and she was able to carry on earning a little surprise for the next week, until her mother felt that she had overcome her worry.

Bowel action is related to diet and well-being, so if your child has loose stools then he is unlikely to be able to control them and a period of reusing a nappy may be necessary. But constipation is the other main problem. A child who has been constipated over a period of time may cause a small anal tear when he passes a motion. This fissure can be painful and it can lead to your child with-holding and becoming more constipated because he is frightened. Retention or 'holding in' of motions can be a problem in young children and they may need a combina-tion of laxative medication and stool softener from your GP, plus a regular positive toilet training regime to en-courage them to pass motions again (Cox *et al.*, 1996). You may see your child sitting on his heel in order to stop the motion coming out. Some children who are severely con-stipated develop 'overflow', which is a leakage of watery stool around the impacted mass in the colon (Kelly, 1996). This can look a bit like watery diarrhoea, but it is not; your GP will be able to tell by pressing your child's abdomen, where he will be able to feel the impacted faeces. Medica-tion is necessary to help this move, but it can be a bit traumatic as your child will suffer tummy pains and feel worried when he thinks it is all about to move. A warm bath can help him relax and, if some of motion comes out in the bath, then don't worry – it is a relaxing place to do it, and it is better out than in.

Looking at your child's diet may be in order if con-stipation is a frequent problem. Prune juice, wholemeal bread, Weetabix, porridge, fruit and vegetables are all ways of helping. But I know that so many young children won't eat these foods. The whole-wheat cereals are prob-ably your best bet if you have a faddy child. In my day cod-liver oil was brilliant for this; but a spoonful of that is pretty hard to take. Lots of exercise and drinking adequate quantities of liquids will keep the bowels working well, and incentives to keep passing motions regularly will keep the throughput regular and easier. If you try to ensure that your child passes a motion at least once every two days then you will help prevent a build-up of constipation again. But excessive anxiety or rigidity about this will cause problems rather than solve them. An incentive programme, like a star chart or small rewards that can be earned for passing a motion in the toilet, can encourage a child to try. Success once a day means that his bowel habits are becoming regular and he will avoid the problem of constipation. But do be careful never to offer rewards for clean pants: this is a perfect recipe for encouraging retention of motions and severe constipation.

Boys again are generally slower in achieving bowel control than girls. During the first 2 years of life, boys and girls soil at the same rate; but the ratio changes to two to three boys for every girl as they grow older (Kelly, 1996). About 88% of 3-year-olds are clean while 98% are clean by age four.

Dry beds

Dry beds are usually attained after your child has achieved daytime dryness – although in some they can occur together. Some children don't begin to achieve this until they are at least 3 years of age. If your child is able to have a dry nappy throughout the night and you are able to get him up in time to go on the early morning potty, then you know that he is ready to manage the night. Some children indicate when they want to stop using a nappy at night, sometimes because their friends have or they want to show how grown-up they are. It may be wise to stop having a bedtime drink, but have it an hour earlier, until you are sure that your child is reliably dry – or you might be tempting fate. Do make sure that you put a plastic sheet under the sheet, just in case.

Some parents lift their child, at about 11 p.m. when they go to bed, in order to ensure a dry night. But you must make sure that your child is fully awake when he goes to the toilet or you are only encouraging bladder release while he is half asleep which is really missing the whole point. The ultimate goal is for him to wake at night when he feels that he wants to go to the toilet. This means that he is responding to the signals from his bladder. Of course, this can at times conflict with a sleeping programme. But you may just have to accept that your child wakes you at night occasionally while he is learning to last out the night.

Sometimes an incentive system, like a star chart for dry beds, can be helpful if the process of training is dragging on a bit unpredictably. This can give your child the added push to try hard to stay dry. The star should be earned in the morning and be given with a lot of praise and congratulations. If you forget about it, or think that it isn't important, then your child will also devalue it and it will not help to motivate him. Your consistency in encouragement and feedback is an essential part of achieving dry beds (Butler, 1998).

The older preschool child may benefit from a 'bell and pad' or 'enuresis alarm' training approach, although it is unlikely that your local clinic will give out the equipment until your child is over 5 years of age. This involves a mat that is placed on the bed. When your child wets at night it sets off an alarm which wakes your child immediately. The aim is for your child to be woken just as his bladder muscles are relaxing so that he learns to recognise the signals from his bladder. You need to get up, make him go to the toilet to empty his bladder, change the bed and reset the alarm. It is quite a lot of effort, and if you ignore the alarm or do not reset it on a dry bed, then your child will not learn effectively how to stay dry. Consistency and effort are needed in order to teach him quickly (Mellon & Houts, 1998).

There are frequent setbacks with night training. Going on holiday, illness or marked changes in routine can easily upset the pattern. Your child may be as distressed as you at finding a wet bed, so don't be too upset, but encourage a dry one the next night. I remember going camping with my young children many years ago and, after a very heavy downpour one night, a pool of water collected in the tent under my 4-year-old's sleeping bag. She was highly indignant when she woke up in the morning and shouted, 'I have not wet my bed!', so that everyone could hear.

Topical tips

- Most children are toilet trained with the utmost of ease.

- Think how difficult it is for you to go to the toilet when someone is shouting at you or telling you to hurry up.

- A child who knows he is in real pants seriously knows that he has to stay dry.

- Incentives and star charts are very effective tools for teaching over-3-year-olds.

- Constipation can lead to fear of passing a motion.

- 'Holding in' of motions will exacerbate constipation.

- Dry beds are achieved when your child wakes up in response to signals from his bladder.

References

Budd, K. S., Chugh, C. S. and Berry, S. I. (1998) 'Parents as therapists for children's food refusal problems', in J. H. Briesmeister and C. E. Schaefer (eds) *Handbook of Parent Training: Parents as Co-therapists for Children's Behaviours* (2nd edn), John Wiley & Sons, New York.

Butler, R. J. (1998) 'Night wetting in children: psychological aspects', *Journal of Child Psychology & Psychiatry*, **39**, 453–65.

Campbell, S. B. (1990) *Behaviour Problems in Pre-school Children: Clinical and Developmental Issues*, Guilford Press, New York.

Campbell, S. B. and Ewing, L. J. (1990) 'Follow-up of hard to manage preschoolers: adjustment at age 9 and predictors of continuing symptoms', *Journal of Child Psychology & Psychiatry*, **31**, 871–91.

Covell, K. and Abramovitch, R. (1987) 'Understanding emotion in the family', *Child Development*, **58**, 985–91.

Cox, D. J., Sutphen, J., Lind, W., Quillian, W. and Borrowitz, S. (1996) 'Additive benefits of laxative, toilet training and biofeedback therapies in the treatment of pediatric encopresis', *Journal of Pediatric Psychology*, **21**, 659–70.

Cummings, E. M. and Davies, P. T. (1994) *Children and Marital Conflict: The Impact of Family Dispute and Resolution*, Guilford Press, New York.

Denham, S. A., McKinley, M., Couchoud, E. A. and Holt, R. (1990)

'Emotional and behavioral prediction of preschool peer ratings', *Child Development*, **61**, 1145–52.

Douglas, J. (1991) *Is My Child Hyperactive?*, Penguin, Harmondsworth.

Douglas, J. E. and Richman, N. (1984) *My Child Won't Sleep*, Penguin, Harmondsworth.

Dowling, E. and Gorell-Barnes, G. (1999) 'Children of divorcing families', *Clinical Child Psychology & Psychiatry*, **4**, 39–51.

Egeland, B., Kalkoske, M., Gottesman, N. and Erickson, M. F. (1990) 'Preschool behaviour problems: stability and factors accounting for change', *Journal of Child Psychology & Psychiatry*, **31**, 891–911.

Forehand, R. L. and McMahon, R. J. (1981) *Helping the Noncompliant Child: A Clinician's Guide to Parent Training*, Guilford, New York.

France, K. G. and Hudson, S. M. (1993) 'Management of infant sleep disturbance: a review', *Clinical Psychology Review*, **13**, 635–47.

Golding, K. (2000) 'Parent management training as an intervention to promote adequate parenting', *Clinical Child Psychology & Psychiatry*, **5**, 357–73.

Von Gontard, A. (1998) 'Day and night wetting in children: a pediatric and child psychiatric perspective', *Journal of Child Psychology & Psychiatry*, **39**, 439–53.

Hay, D. F., Castle, J., Davies, L., Demetriou, H. and Stimson, C. A. (1999) 'Prosocial action in very early childhood', *Journal of Child Psychology & Psychiatry*, **40**, 905–16.

Hetherington, E. M. and Stanley-Hagan, M. (1999) 'The adjustment of children with divorced parents: a risk and resiliency perspective', *Journal of Child Psychology & Psychiatry*, **40**, 129–40.

Holden, G. W. (1983) 'Avoiding conflict: mothers as tacticians in the supermarket', *Child Development*, **54**, 233–40.

Jenkins, J. M. and Buccioni, J. M. (2000) 'Children's understanding of marital conflict and the marital relationship', *Journal of Child Psychology & Psychiatry*, **41**, 161–9.

Kelly, C. (1996) 'Chronic constipation and soiling in children: a review of the psychological and family literature', *Child Psychology & Psychiatry Review*, **1**, 59–67.

Landy, S. and Menna, R. (2001) 'Play between aggressive young children and their mothers', *Clinical Child Psychology & Psychiatry*, **6**, 223–41.

Mellon, M. N. and Houts, A. C. (1998) 'Home based treatment for primary enuresis', in J. H. Briesmeister and C. E. Schaefer (eds), *Handbook of Parent Training: Parents as Co-therapists for Children's Behaviours* (2nd edn), John Wiley & Sons, New York.

Pagani, L., Boulerice, B., Tremblay, R. E. and Vitaro, F. (1997) 'Behavioural development in children of divorce and remarriage', *Journal of Child Psychology & Psychiatry*, **38**, 769–81.

Patterson, G. R. (1982) *Coercive Family Process*, Castalia, Eugene, Oregon.

Shure, M. B. and Spivak, G. (1978) *Problem Solving Techniques in Child Rearing*, Jossey-Bass, San Francisco.

Stores, G. (1996) 'Assessment and treatment of sleep disorders in children and adolescents', *Journal of Child Psychiatry & Psychology*, **37**, 907–27.

Webster-Stratton, C. and Hammond, M. (1999) 'Marital conflict management skills, parenting style, and early onset conduct problems: processes and pathways', *Journal of Child Psychology & Psychiatry*, **40**, 917–29.

Webster-Stratton, C. and Hancock, L. (1998) 'Parent training for parents of young children with conduct problems: content, methods and therapeutic process', in J. H. Briesmeister and C. R. Schaefer (eds), *Handbook of Parent Training: Parents as Co-therapists for Children's Behaviours* (2nd edn), John Wiley & Sons, New York.

Webster-Stratton, C. and Herbert, M. (1994) *Troubled Families– Problem Children: Working with Parents. A Collaborative Process*, John Wiley & Sons, Chichester, UK.

Winnicott, D. (1998) *Babies and Their Mothers*, Free Association Books, London.

Woodward, L., Taylor, E. and Dowdney, L. (1998) 'The parenting and family functioning of children with hyperactivity', *Journal of Child Psychology & Psychiatry*, **39**, 161–71.

Wolfson, A. R. (1998) 'Working with parents on developing efficacious sleep/wake habits for infants and young children', in J. H. Briesmeister and C. E. Schaefer (eds), *Handbook of Parent Training: Parents as Co-therapists for Children's Behaviours* (2nd edn), John Wiley & Sons, New York.

Index